HEGEL ON HAMANN

Topics in Historical Philosophy

General Editors David Kolb
John McCumber

Associate Editor Anthony J. Steinbock

HEGEL ON HAMANN

Translated from the German
and with an introduction
by Lisa Marie Anderson

Northwestern University Press
Evanston, Illinois

Northwestern University Press
www.nupress.northwestern.edu

Printed in the United States of America

10   9   8   7   6   5   4   3   2   1

Library of Congress Cataloging-in-Publication Data

Hegel, Georg Wilhelm Friedrich, 1770–1831.
   [Hamann's Schriften. English]
   Hegel on Hamann / translated from the German by Lisa Marie Anderson.
     p. cm.—(Topics in historical philosophy)
   Includes bibliographical references and index.
   ISBN-13: 978-0-8101-2492-9 (cloth : alk. paper)
   ISBN-10: 0-8101-2492-0 (cloth : alk. paper)
   ISBN-13: 978-0-8101-2491-2 (pbk. : alk. paper)
   ISBN-10: 0-8101-2491-2 (pbk. : alk. paper)
   1. Hamann, Johann Georg, 1730–1788. Hamann's Schriften. 2. Hamann,
Johann Georg, 1730–1788—Criticism and interpretation. 3. Hegel, Georg
Wilhelm Friedrich, 1770–1831—Criticism and interpretation. 4. Germany—
Intellectual life—18th century. I. Anderson, Lisa Marie. II. Title. III. Series:
Northwestern University topics in historical philosophy.
B2993.H4413 2008
193—dc22
                                         2008007025

For Ed, who knows why words fail

Contents

Note on the Text

G. W. F. Hegel's essay "Hamanns Schriften" ("The Writings of Hamann") originally appeared in the *Jahrbücher für wissenschaftliche Kritik* (*Yearbooks for Scientific Criticism*) in October and December 1828, nos. 77–80 and 107–14. It was a review of J. G. Hamann's collected works, which had appeared under the editorship of Friedrich Roth in 1821–25. The review includes two footnotes by Hegel, which stand as footnotes in the translation. My translator's notes appear as endnotes. All translations in this volume are my own, unless I have specified otherwise either expressly or in the bibliographic information in the notes. For other translations of Hamann, see those by James C. O'Flaherty, Ronald Gregor Smith, Gwen Griffith Dickson, and Kenneth Haynes, listed in the bibliography under the heading "Primary Sources in English (Translations, Commentaries)."

In translating Hegel's review, I have retained many of his textual practices, including his frequent and often idiosyncratic use of italics for emphasis. Where Hegel includes phrases in Greek, Latin, or French in his text (often in a quote from Hamann), I have left them as such, and translated only the Greek phrases in the notes.

In other cases, I have chosen to standardize some elements of Hegel's text. His use of punctuation, for example, makes many long and complex sentences quite difficult to decipher, and I have tried to address this. Moreover, Hegel makes numerous references to a volume and/or page number in the Roth (R) edition of Hamann's collected works, the edition he is reviewing. While these references stand in the translation, I have standardized and expanded them somewhat, and supplemented them in the notes with the corresponding reference in the newer and more widely accepted Nadler (N) edition or, in the case of Hamann's letters, the Ziesemer/Henkel edition (ZH). As Hegel notes, the letters which make up Hamann's extensive correspondence with F. H. Jacobi were not included in the Roth edition, so Hegel references them from Jacobi's correspondence; I have retained and standardized these references. All of Hegel's references, however, are given less than consistently, and where they are missing from his text, I have provided them, with volume and page numbers for the available editions, in the notes. I reference both the Roth and the more recent editions of Hamann in the other parts of this volume as well. Where I reference my translation of Hegel's essay in these supplemental sections of the book, I do so with the abbreviation *HH,* short for *Hegel on Hamann,* and cite the page numbers of the present volume.

Hegel's text and the Hamann quotations embedded within it quote from the Bible at numerous points, always from the Luther translation of 1545. I have generally used either the New Revised Standard Version or the King James Version in my translation of these quotes, but have also remained as close as possible to the Luther translation, since many of its words and phrases correspond directly to deliberate choices Hamann makes in his works and letters.

Hegel is known for the considerable license he takes when quoting others. This manifests itself in different ways in his review of Hamann. First, some of the "quotations" in this text actually represent Hegel's accurate paraphrase of Hamann, in which case I have not added anything to the text. Second, Hegel frequently lifts phrases directly from Hamann and others (e.g., Goethe, Mendelssohn) without any indication; this I have attempted to indicate in my notes with a reference to the source. Finally, in cases of inaccurate or significantly incomplete paraphrases of Hamann (some of which may be attributable to the editions which Hegel had at hand), I have translated the text written by Hegel so as to convey his intentions and have indicated divergences from Hamann's text by way of comparison in the notes.

This volume begins with two introductory essays which I hope will facilitate and contextualize the reader's experience of the translation. The first provides a general overview of Hegel's review and Hamann's position in eighteenth-century thought. The second focuses specifically on the notion of friendship, a cornerstone of Hegel's text only in part because of its centrality in the intellectual culture of the age. Friendship is also, in this case, a category which facilitates a better understanding of Hegel's often stark critique of Hamann's personal and authorial development.

Acknowledgments

I am grateful to the faculty and administration of Duke University and Hunter College, City University of New York, for affording me the time and flexibility to complete this book, and to my colleagues in German at both institutions for their feedback and encouragement as its ideas developed and crystallized. For sparking my initial interest in Hamann and many of the subjects in this book, I am indebted to the faculty in the German department at the University of Pennsylvania.

For their excellent suggestions about the manuscript, I thank the readers and editorial staff at Northwestern University Press. I am especially grateful to John McCumber and Henry Carrigan for their help with the project. I also greatly appreciate the permission of the Felix Meiner Verlag to reprint some of the material in this volume.

I thank my family as always for their support of this and all my other endeavors over the years. Without it, none of my work would be possible.

Finally, it would be difficult to overstate the debt of gratitude I owe to Eddis Miller for his support of this project, from its original unearthing through its completion. The introductory essays in particular have benefited from his insights and expertise. Most of all, I am extremely fortunate to have had such a careful and thoughtful reader, listener, and dialogue partner, and I thank him for his uniquely inspirational wisdom, unwavering encouragement, and invaluable friendship.

Introduction

Johann Georg Hamann died in 1788, two months shy of his fifty-eighth birthday. It would be another thirty-three years before his collected works began to appear, under the editorship of Friedrich Roth.[1] Once all of Hamann's writings had come out, Georg Wilhelm Friedrich Hegel published a review of them in the *Jahrbücher für wissenschaftliche Kritik* (*Yearbooks for Scientific Criticism*), discussing at length, among other things, the circumstances which had hindered their earlier appearance.[2] This was late in 1828, during Hegel's Berlin period and just three years before his own death. His review, then, represents a rare gem in the history of German thought: the musings of the mature Hegel, the most important German philosopher of the post-Enlightenment period, on one of the most enigmatic writers in European history, whose work had been or would be so influential for such well-known thinkers as Herder, Jacobi, Goethe, and Kierkegaard, but whose meaning remained hidden and in need of explication to a great number of his readers.

Hegel's review essay has been translated into French and Italian.[3] That the present volume contains its first ever translation into English is all the more surprising given the recent resurgence of interest in Hamann on the part of scholars of literature, religious studies, theology, and philosophy. This resurgence is well warranted given the range of interests to which Hamann's work speaks in such unique ways. We will rehash here neither Hamann's biography (which Hegel recounts in such detail in the review itself) nor what a previous wave of Hamann scholarship has offered about such diverse topics as his supposedly irrationalist or antirationalist opposition to the Enlightenment, his conception of genius and its impact on the Sturm und Drang movement, his influence on existentialism, or even his radical—for his time—views on sexuality.[4] More recently, Gwen Griffith Dickson has offered a new and in many ways revolutionary picture of Hamann's thought, focusing on his hermeneutical method and his concern with textuality (both of which, Dickson shows, prefigure both modernist and postmodernist thought, from Wittgenstein to Rorty).[5] For those unfamiliar with Hamann scholarship both old and new, a bibliography is provided at the end of this volume, with special focus on works written in English. This volume, though, focuses on Hegel's essay and what it tells us about Hamann, about the time in which he lived and wrote. As radically different as the two men are, this text in which their paths cross, as it were, yields insights not only about Hamann but about the mature Hegel as well, and about the legacy of eighteenth- and nineteenth-century philosophy in Germany.

Hegel's review itself is often perplexing, from its apparently excessive concern with Hamann's personal life—even accounting for Hegel's belief that Hamann's "individuality" is the key to understanding his writings, and that Hamann's (semi)autobiographical writings represent the "principal novelty" of the Roth edition (*HH*, 7)—to the portions of that life and of Hamann's works which Hegel omits completely from his account, to the sometimes extremely harsh criticisms he levels at Hamann.[6] Isaiah Berlin and others have come away with the impression that Hegel's review is "not too friendly,"[7] but I find Dickson's characterization of the essay as "a certain qualified stamp of approval"[8] most apt. Hamann does seem to have won Hegel's approval on a number of points, including, on a personal level, his undying devotion to his friendships, and his ability to learn from experience. But this approval could not have been other than "qualified" in light of Hegel's "requirements" not for private individuals but "for philosophy and philosophers";[9] of course, the proudly systematic Hegel easily found fault with a thinker who defined "the heroic spirit of a philosopher" as "a thirsting ambition for truth and virtue, and a fury to conquer all lies and vices which are not recognized as such, nor wish to be" (R 2:16–17; N 2:63), and who felt himself "pleasantly compelled to fumigate the fashionable spirit of my century with doubts" (R 4:48; N 3:41).

Still, it may be difficult to conclude on the basis of this text whether or not Hegel thoroughly failed to understand Hamann. His review remains quite focused on the beginning and end of Hamann's literary career. Josef Nadler, author of the definitive Hamann biography in German, and editor of the historical-critical edition of his works, even believes it possible that Hegel read none of what Hamann wrote between the *Socratic Memorabilia* (1759) and *Golgotha and Sheblimini* (1784).[10] It may rather be the case that Hegel chose to discuss primarily these two texts—along with the *Metacritique* on Kant, written in 1784—because they represent the apex of Hamann's literary production. Either way, Hegel's review of Hamann's works is by no means exhaustive, and its reader is left wishing that he had had more to say about, for example, *Aesthetica in nuce*, or the *Essay of a Sibyl on Marriage*. Perhaps it is most accurate to say that Hegel did not make a sustained attempt to understand Hamann on his own terms.

Stephen Dunning attributes this lack of understanding, whatever its nature, to a fundamental "difference" between the two men about the nature of *language*.[11] As so many commentators have noted, this is a category that underlies all of Hamann's thought, diverse as its topics are. Most interesting for the purposes of this volume is the point at which Hamann's view of language centers around the idea of translation. Speaking itself, he writes in *Aesthetica in nuce* (1760), "is translation—from a language of angels into a language of men, that is, thoughts into words—things into names—images into signs" (R 2:262; N 2:199). Anticipating the work of Walter Benjamin (who acknowledges Hamann's influence, despite their differences, in "On Language," and might well have in "The Task of the Translator"), Hamann suggests that language is itself translation, and that human language is inextricable from its particular relationship to a more divine predecessor. Hamann believes that only by understanding language as such are humans able to name, and thus to hope to perceive, things or images.

Yet Hamann's particular attunement to language remains relatively underappreciated in Hegel's review. Hegel seems concerned with Hamann's view of language as such only in his analysis of Hamann's objection to the Kantian critical project. Indeed, Hegel could not have done any less with language in this part of his review, since Hamann identifies it as simultaneously the "only, first, and last organon and criterion of reason," "the crux of the *misunderstanding* of reason with itself," and the basis of our very faculty of thought. The problem with Kant's critical idealism, to paraphrase Hamann, is its mischievous attempt to purify language from transmission and tradition, to reduce it to a dishonest system of "hieroglyphics and types" (*HH*, 37), to manipulate it until it is arbitrary and elusive. Hamann's insistence on unity, in defiance of Kantian divisions, depends ultimately on his conviction that words belong indivisibly to both sensibility/intuition and understanding/concepts. With the exception of this necessary and limited synopsis, though, Hegel seems more interested, often derisively so, in the language Hamann uses than in his understanding of the concept of language itself. Hegel's review offers almost nothing, for example, on the substance (as opposed to the personal circumstances) of Hamann's writings on Herder (*Herderschriften*), in which he worked through his own theory of language in response to his friend's prizewinning and now-seminal essay on the origin of language.

This relative disregard on Hegel's part is all the more surprising given that Hamann's understanding of language is so clearly essential for his views on religion (and vice versa, as we have seen), which *are* a real focal point for Hegel. That all of Hamann's writings are so thoroughly infused with biblical language is surely a direct consequence of the fact that Hamann's religious turn was inspired, as Hegel details, by his reading of the Bible. Subsequent to that very personal experience during a stay in London, often described as a conversion or, in keeping with Hamann's Lutheran convictions, a "tower experience" (*Turmerlebnis*),[12] Hamann developed more universal ideas as to how scripture should be read and interpreted, ideas which are encapsulated in the statement to Jacobi which Hegel recounts: "All clinging to words and literal teachings of religion is *Lama-Worship*" (*HH,* 29). This too is a conviction which Hegel considers primarily with regard to Hamann's counter-Enlightenment tendencies. For Hamann, exegesis depends on, in Hegel's words, "a positive foundation" which is not "a doctrinal formula contained in literal words (as in the literal faith of orthodoxy)" but rather "only the beginning of his faith, essential to its animating application, for its formation, expression, and concretization." Further, Hamann's confidence that "this animating principle is essentially [one's] own individual spirit" leads to his chastisement of "the so-called Enlightening [*die Aufklärerei*] which had the impudence to boast of the authority of the letter which it alone could *interpret.*" Hamann continued to insist instead that "the *meaning* which exegesis brings is also an understood, subjective meaning" (*HH,* 30). This strain of Hamann's thought, at least, must have met with sympathy from Hegel, who had written in his *Lectures on the Philosophy of Religion* (just the year before the Hamann review appeared) the following about biblical exegesis: "One does not take the words as they stand, because what is understood by the biblical 'word' is not words or letters as such but the spirit with which they are grasped."[13]

Although Hegel can use the word "orthodoxy" to describe Hamann's religiosity at various points in his essay, he is careful to define, with recourse to religious history and contemporary debates, what orthodoxy may and may not mean in Hamann's case. It is "his Christian orthodoxy" which separates Hamann from "the Berlin Enlightenment," at least, but Hegel insists that Hamann's is not "the wooden, orthodox theology of his time" (*HH,* 6), not "a faith which a person carries inside himself only as a dead formula, external to the spirit and the heart" (29). Instead, Hegel says, Hamann's "spirit retains the highest freedom" (6).

If Hegel stands in relative agreement with Hamann on the subject of exegesis and does not condemn his particular brand of orthodoxy, then the source of his indictment of Hamann's religiosity must lie elsewhere. Indeed, each time Hegel accuses Hamann of pious hypocrisy or isolated subjectivity (the two pillars of Hegel's critique in this regard), he is taking issue specifically with Hamann's understanding of the nature of salvation or of God himself. The first sign of hypocrisy Hegel identifies is Hamann's "application" of the forgiveness he attained via salvation to the forgiveness of his monetary debts, that is, his assurance that God will take care of the matter as an excuse not to make payment himself (*HH,* 13). The other hypocrisy that results, according to Hegel, from Hamann's conversion is that "he, having absolved himself inwardly of his sins, now not only pesters his friends with the confession that he is the greatest of sinners, but further answers to them for his starving, directionless, and lazy lifestyle with the pantheism of false religiosity, namely that it is all God's will" (27). While such irresponsible behavior on Hamann's part is in itself certainly distasteful, far more serious for Hegel is the perspective that underlies it, which reduces Christian salvation to a mere "comfort" for Hamann from the "perception of his weakness" (16).

Hegel takes more seriously still the manner in which Hamann "isolates himself" in the "fortress" of "his penitence and the faith he has attained via divine grace." This isolation allows Hamann to spurn "the conditions of reality" and the "objective principles" of others, to claim "superiority over so-called earthly duties" (*HH,* 15), and leaves him trapped in "an abstract interiority whose stubborn simplicity neither recognizes objective regulations, duties, or theoretical or practical principles as essential per se, nor takes the slightest interest in these things" (25). Thus any "spiritual depth" which Hegel is able to praise in Hamann "lingers in completely concentrated intensity and arrives at no sort of expansion, be it in fantasy or in thought" (31). This, then, is the reason Hegel feels compelled to concern so much of his review with Hamann's personal life and individual convictions; these are what inform and indeed hopelessly constrain Hamann's philosophy and thus his writings. Hence Hegel's characterization of "Hamann's authorial character" as confined to "the expression of [his] personal singularity," at the grave expense of "an objective content" (31).

All of these characteristics of Hamann's religiosity and spirituality (in a Hegelian sense) fly in the face of what Hegel believes about spirit, God, and revelation. Drawing on a metaphor Hamann himself has borrowed, Hegel describes God as a "balled core of truth" which has, in a revelatory act, unfolded itself "into a system of nature, into a system of the state, of justice and morality, into a system of world history" (*HH,* 39).[14] Revelation is seen here as anything but personal, and as such it requires that one "enter into this unfolding by way of reflection *on* it"; this "is both the purpose and the express duty of thinking spirit in and of itself" (39). By Hegel's standards, Hamann's spirit refused to overcome its "concentration" and take part in God's revelation in this manner, which rendered him necessarily indifferent to "doctrines of truth" as well as "moral commandments and legal duties" (40). In other words, Hamann's relationship to God, like most aspects of his life and thought, is too "limited to subjective feeling and imagination" for Hegel's tastes, too eager to immerse itself helplessly into "the mysteries of previous, partial revelations" rather than the fullness of revelation in Christ.[15]

The final piece of Hamann's views on religion which must be examined here is the role of faith. Hegel's ruminations on this subject are a part of his discussion of Hamann's *Socratic Memorabilia*. Hegel does not mention the influence of David Hume in this context, though Hamann wrote to Jacobi years later that he had been "full of Hume" when he wrote the *Memorabilia* (ZH 7:167). Manfred Kuehn has shown how Hamann uses Hume to argue that "philosophy can only lead to skepticism, and skepticism leads to belief." The step from "belief" to "faith" is, as Kuehn notes, one which Hamann could not have made without the double meaning of *Glaube* in German, which can signify either "belief" (from the verb *glauben*) or "faith."[16] Hegel sees it as a step in the other direction, with the "broad claim which religious faith has only in the right and power of its absolute content" being "expanded to subjective believing with the particularity and haphazardness of its relative and finite content." In the *Memorabilia*, Hegel says, "statements about *faith*" are "extended to a universal sense, such that the *sensory certainty* of outward, temporal things— 'of our own being and of the existence of all things'—is also called a *faith*." Hegel continues with the observation that it is just this "extension" which characterizes what became better known as "*Jacobi's* principle of faith" (in which one is actually reading Hamann "almost verbatim") (*HH,* 20). While the principle of expansion or extension might seem to indicate that Hamann's thought is moving closer to Hegel's expectations here, Hegel's insistence upon "the particularity and haphazardness" of believing (as opposed to faith), which can have only a "relative and finite content," demonstrates that he does not consider Hamann to have moved beyond his characteristic shortcomings here after all.

If Hegel leaves Hume more or less out of the analysis here, his essay is filled with and in fact grounds itself upon references to Christian Wolff. Hegel even seems to suggest, having taken pains to show that Hamann's thought is actually unfit for the real task of philosophy, that Hamann was *forced* to deal with philosophy at all because "the theological drive of his time is immediately connected . . . first and foremost, to Wolffian philosophy" (*HH*, 35). Hamann's *Golgotha and Sheblimini*, for example, depends on a rejection of the Wolffian principles which are the underpinnings of Moses Mendelssohn's *Jerusalem*. As for Hegel, he begins his review by characterizing the Wolffian philosophy of the time as "a methodical, sober form" for expressing "thought," which became as devoid of "spirituality" as of "originality." Enlightenment in the Wolffian mold, according to Hegel, "consisted solely in establishing now in Germany the principles of deism, religious tolerance, and morality which *Rousseau* and *Voltaire* had raised to the general way of thinking among the upper classes in and beyond France." This brand of enlightenment, based in Berlin (read: Nicolai, Mendelssohn, the *Allgemeine Deutsche Bibliothek*), "was pursued with dry understanding, with principles of bald utility, with insipidity of spirit and knowledge, paltry or ordinary passions, and, where it was most respectable, with some (albeit sober) warmth of feeling." Hegel differentiates from this Wolffian enlightening the version which was practiced outside Berlin by Kant, Lessing, Jacobi, and others (including Hamann) "whose depth was in poetry as well as in thinking reason." Hegel has far more praise for this group of his predecessors, a veritable "wreath of original individualities." Among them, Hamann in particular is considered a true original (*ein Original*). This characterization, however, like so many in Hegel's review, turns almost immediately from an ostensible compliment into a lament, in this case of Hamann's "deep particularity, which proved incapable not only of any form of universality, but also of the expansion of thinking reason as a matter of taste" (4–6).

As Hegel repeatedly suggests, it was the formidable task of deciphering this originality that prevented Hamann from being as widely read as his contemporaries. Still, this originality (likely the very factor which had inspired Hegel to write his review in the first place) certainly influenced, and would continue to influence, a number of thinkers who were prepared to read Hamann on his own terms, subjectivist and intensely personal though they might be. For its part, Hegel's review continues to serve as an important introduction to the life and works of Hamann. Any bias its limitations might instill in an audience generally unfamiliar with Hamann is easily remedied by further readings, and is moreover outweighed by Hegel's elucidation and philosophical contextualization of Hamann's thought, which is as welcome to Hamann scholars as to those just beginning to grapple with his work.

The Notion of Friendship in Hegel and Hamann

In her book *Johann Georg Hamann's Relational Metacriticism,* Gwen Griffith Dickson suggests that "the key to understanding Hamann's approach to" "language, knowledge, and anthropology" "can be found in the idea of the relationship," both "the first and foundational . . . human-divine relationship that . . . grounds all being, knowledge and language" and "the relations of one human being to another" which are in fact "no less crucial."[1] In this introductory essay, I would like to focus on a specific kind of relationship which played an absolutely central role in Hamann's life and, as Hegel stresses, in the genesis and development of his authorship: friendship.

Hegel's review devotes a surprising amount of attention to Hamann's personal life. Within Hegel's consideration of Hamann's biography and personality, the bond of friendship is even more essential than are familial ties. Hegel's treatment of Hamann's friendships—and of the very notion of friendship, a vitalizing "life-pulse" (*HH,* 45) for Hamann—becomes a recurring theme and is in some passages quite thoroughgoing. Thus, it seems fitting to consider the role that friendship plays not only in Hegel's review and Hamann's life, but also in the thought of both men, and in the eighteenth and early nineteenth centuries in Germany.

Hamann has been described as having a "singular capacity for friendship"[2] and a "convivial character" that made him "the epicenter of a circle of friends."[3] He has even been called "a genius of friendship," full of "an insatiable desire for . . . communication."[4] Hegel himself notes the general importance of friendship "in the affairs of the scholars and literati" (*HH,* 25) of Hamann's time.[5] But his sustained attention to Hamann's friendships has still another impetus; it is in large part attributable to the fact that Hamann's friendships cannot be separated from his life as a thinker and writer. For one thing, many of Hamann's writings were dedicated to and in fact written for his friends, some of them even qualifying as what in German is called *Gelegenheitsdichtung,* something written for a quite specific occasion. His *Essay of a Sibyl on Marriage* (1775), to cite just one example among many, was a gift for his friend, the Riga bookseller and publisher Johann Friedrich Hartknoch, upon his marriage to Albertine Toussaint. Publication, too, was bound up with Hamann's friendships; most of his works "were published as a courtesy."[6] Hegel indicates that Hamann's friends also helped him at times to overcome his inherently unproductive, even lazy, wasteful nature. Almost any employment Hamann ever held or hoped to hold, he came to through the urging or the assistance of a friend, be it the statesman Karl Friedrich von Moser or even Hamann's fellow Königsberger, Immanuel Kant.[7] And when this employment turned out to be less than lucrative, Hamann depended on subsidies from friends like Johann Gottfried Herder (without whose financial assistance he would have had to sell his library) or Franz von Buchholtz.[8]

Hamann's letters contain a veritable collection of often aphoristic views about friendship. He writes in 1758 that "one single friend outweighs all the treasures of India" (R 1:297; ZH 1:249). He calls friends "a gift from God" (R 1:379; ZH 1:324) and friendship "a fruit of the spirit which is also called *Friend* and Comforter" (R 1:391; ZH 1:338). This is just one of the many declarations in which Hamann demonstrates the connection between his Christianity and his human friendships.[9] He writes to his close friend Johann Gotthelf Lindner: "He whom we do not see, even if he is with us, in us and among us, He who fills the room, who separates us two from another, wants our hearts to hear his greeting: 'Peace be with you!' wants to send us about his business and his Father's, and wants to help us lead our whole lives with the dignity and truth of his messenger whom he has sent" (R 1:391; ZH 1:338). Continuing in the biblical reference which pervades all his work, Hamann writes later of "the daily bread of friendship" (R 1:500; ZH 1:436), and calls it later still the "salt and seasoning for our daily bread . . . by which alone man does not live" (R 7:142; ZH 5:167).

This conceptual link between Hamann's friendships and his Christianity developed during the period he spent in London, a tumultuous and formative time which was just that, Hamann says in his *Thoughts About My Life,* because he found himself then utterly without friends. In London, he writes, "I always prayed to God for a friend, for a wise, honest friend . . . Instead, I had tasted quite enough of the gall of false friendship . . . A friend who could give me a key to my heart, the guide for my labyrinth—this was a wish I wished frequently, without really understanding or appreciating its content." Hamann goes on to describe the moment in which his wish was fulfilled: "Praise God! I found this friend in my heart, creeping into it as I felt most of all the emptiness and darkness and the desert of my heart" (R 1:210; N 2:39–40). It is Hamann's reading of the Bible to which he connects this moment so characteristic of eighteenth-century Pietism and sensibility (*Empfindsamkeit*), finding the desired friend in his heart, in the person of Christ.

Perhaps the clearest statement of the connection Hamann draws between his earthly friendships and his intensely personal Christianity is the passage he quotes, in a letter to his brother, from Saint John Chrysostom:

> Make friends to the glory of God. . . . If we do not win such friends as through whom we acquire riches, at whose table we may savor, and through whom we may become mighty, then we ought to seek them out and make them our friends who keep our souls always in order, who admonish us to fulfill our duties, who punish us when we sin, who prop us up when we stumble, and who support us with prayer and counsel, in order to bring us to God. (R 1:500–501; ZH 1:436)

Clearly, Hamann understands friendship not only as a blessing but also as a reciprocal obligation or, more accurately, a series of obligations requiring extreme watchfulness and frankness. He writes to his brother of "all the attentiveness, honesty and affection . . . which good friends owe each other, even if they feel compelled to live according to different schemata [*Entwürfe*]" (R 1:500; ZH 1:436), as Hamann and his friends often did. "True friendship," he believes, requires "deliberation, self-denial, sacrifice, a cool head, a fiery heart" (R 7:156–57; ZH 5:182).

For Hamann, friendship and its trials are so important precisely because they are an essential part of the human path toward self-knowledge, a path along which friends, by definition, have a duty to help each other. But this strong sense of duty and even obligation in friendship becomes considerably more delicate when it casts friends into the roles of teacher and pupil or master and disciple. Where it seems to many that Hamann is not only a friend but is also, as Diane Morgan puts it, the "worst enemy who exposes your faults relentlessly and punishes you for your vanity and superciliousness," and is "insultingly direct and critical in the name of a friendship which is projected into the future as an agonistic model for successive generations," Hamann believes he is doing only his duty in speaking the truth to his friends, despite the risk of injuring them.[10] "To know one's friends," he writes to Johann Friedrich Reichardt, "is the ground of all duties toward them, difficult, painstaking, fastidious like self-knowledge—and indispensable for its progress" (R 6:287; ZH 4:432). This is why Hamann can claim that "friendship, like all our virtues, is basically grounded in human weakness" (R 6:290; ZH 4:435).

This conception of friendship is played out in Hamann's life and writings in two seemingly contradictory ways. On the one hand, Hamann's friend Johann Georg Scheffner once wrote that "without wishing to teach others," Hamann "had a great influence on the spirit of his young friends, which was very advantageous for them."[11] Scheffner is likely thinking here of the Hamann who wrote to Lindner in 1759 that friendship has nothing to do "with teaching, instructing, repenting or proselytizing." "Can there be any question here," he asks, "of teaching or instructing?" He continues sarcastically: "Good friend, be good enough not to lie, and do not boast, and don't do this and that. . . . Speak volumes to your friend, instruct him, confute him; you will show that you are a learned, reasonable, clever man, but what interest does friendship have in all these acts?" (R 1:474–75; ZH 1:405).

This Hamann stands in marked contrast to the man more frequently reflected in his writings, to the often condescending personality which made it impossible for Hegel and others to agree with Scheffner that Hamann did not wish to teach his friends. One of these others was Goethe, who has quite a bit to say, in his autobiography, about both Hamann's career and Hamann as a man and friend, though he never met Hamann or corresponded with him.[12] After reading his "excellent" correspondence, Goethe concluded that Hamann was "very clear-headed about his situation and life and his friendships," with "sure instincts about the relationships of people to each other and to him." But Goethe also took from these letters that Hamann, "very naively conscious of his superior intellectual gifts, always considered himself somewhat wiser and cleverer than his correspondents, whom he addressed with more irony than cordiality." This, Goethe says, is precisely why he "never desired a closer contact with [Hamann]."[13]

To begin to trace the attitude Goethe is talking about, we can return to the very same letter to Lindner cited above, in which Hamann also writes: "We owe friends more than any others the most attentiveness; so when we instruct them, we must carry out this instruction with more attentiveness than any other" (R 1:473–74; ZH 1:405). Later, Hamann will encourage his own son to put great stock in "the school of friendship": "Knowledge swells us up, but love improves us and its anointing teaches us everything. We do not owe our happiness to the tree of knowledge. There is a better, a higher way than tongues and gnosticism. So apply the school of friendship well, and it will contribute more than any other to your education and upbringing" (R 6:362; ZH 5:104). The contradiction is apparent, between the assertion on the one hand (largely the product of Hamann's Pietist background) that friendships necessarily include reciprocal instruction, so that my friend and I, as "each other's confessors and ministers,"[14] may be continually improving our souls through each other, and on the other hand that teaching has no place in friendship.

How to reconcile this contradiction, all the more strange because it takes shape not over the course of Hamann's life and development, but within a single letter? It is possible that this issue of instructing one's friends represents Hamann's greatest personal hypocrisy, mingled with false modesty and some defensiveness in the letter to Lindner. Hegel seems to conclude as much when he writes of Hamann's "sanctimonious language and the contrarious tone which tended more toward the language of hypocrisy than toward piety" (*HH*, 27). But behind this hypocrisy lies a tension in which Hamann persisted throughout his life, between a sincere desire to assist his friends, to tell them the truth in order to help them "along toward self-knowledge," and an undeniable drive "to be recognized as a teacher and a prophet" (17–18). This tension is best explained by a category which Hegel invokes in numerous contexts within his essay, namely Hamann's parrhesia.[15] What Hamann thought about this rhetorical form—famously defined by Michel Foucault as one in which the speaker courageously "says everything he has in mind" and "opens his heart and mind completely to other people," both in the interest of absolute truth and to inspire those people to change[16]—surely came from his knowledge of both the classics, where Plato casts Socrates in the role of the parrhesiast, and the New Testament, where Paul, for example, uses the term repeatedly. Hamann adopts Pauline rhetoric to characterize himself "with the parrhesia of confession and admission" as "the noblest of sinners" (16), an exercise which Hegel seems to regard as false piety and perhaps even a grave misunderstanding of the nature of salvation. Though Hamann's parrhesia more frequently serves to rebuke his friends for their sins and to urge them to change, the dual purpose of this mode of speech demonstrates that he saw himself as a confessor in both senses of the term: as one who makes a confession, and as one who hears and accepts such a confession, in this case having inspired or demanded it himself.

Of course, as Peter Fenves points out, "even if the relation between master and disciples can still be called friendship, the former is a friend of an entirely different order."[17] Thus Hamann's frankness necessarily put his friendships at risk, jeopardizing as it did any sense of comfortable assurance among equals.[18] While Hamann never completely mastered the basic drive in his nature which seemed to prevent him from treating his friends as his equals, there is evidence that he became increasingly aware of the resentment it stirred up in them, and of their reticence to engage him in it. Even Hegel, whose disdain is apparent when he says that Hamann was not "in the habit of whispering his parrhesia" (*HH*, 29), admits that Hamann did make some progress in this regard. Still, Hamann's life and authorship are shaped by his early desire "to help his friends to self-knowledge by scolding them for their every failing," which "produced a series of wrecked relationships, which Hegel recounts in several places and at painful length."[19] This being the case, we will not spend more time recounting the circumstances of these relationships here than is needed to round out our portrait of friendship—and the central friends—in Hamann's life.

"Alcibiades and Socrates": Kant and Berens

As we have noted, a new understanding of friendship, and thus of the path to self-knowledge, developed in Hamann during his stay in London. He had been sent there as an employee of the Berens family, merchants in Riga. Hamann had befriended one of the Berens brothers, Johann Christoph, at university. Returning to Riga from London, Hamann found himself somewhat at odds with old friends like Berens on account of his "conversion," prior to which he seems to have shared their Enlightenment values to a much greater degree. In fact, Berens went to great efforts to win Hamann back to the cause of reason once Hamann had chosen to ground his life and thought in the principle of faith instead, even enlisting the help of mutual friends like Lindner and Kant. In formulating epistolary responses to their efforts, Hamann encountered immediately the tension between being a friend and being a critical teacher of self-knowledge, since he did not stop at defending his own position, but wished moreover to convert his friends to it. This conflict led to an extremely difficult time, if not a breakdown, in Hamann's friendship with Berens and with Kant. Hegel claims that this "struggle and squabble" is so formative as to be the "origination" of Hamann's "entire individuality, manner of representation, and style" (*HH*, 14–15).

Hegel believes that this "individuality" is grounded in an "inner confidence" which prevents Hamann from submitting to his friends' demands that he be reasonable and "respect their objective principles." What is more, Hamann uses this fixed position to "turn the tables" on his friends and demand "penance and conversion" from them (*HH*, 15). He does so in letters that become quite haughty, as he sees the whole debate as an opportunity for God, working through him, to save the souls of his friends. He compares his friends' rejection of his demands to the rejection Christ suffered, and considers himself similarly misunderstood by those around him. In Hamann's understanding of friendship, the entire disagreement is actually a divine gift, a test meant to improve the souls of all involved. But it seems Hamann fails to see how the superior position he occupies in this test makes it a supremely distasteful one for his friends.

Paralleling himself with Christ is not the only way Hamann expresses his superiority in the matter. Here and throughout his work, in fact, a typological relationship emerges between classical and Christian thought, with Socrates prefiguring Christ. This is already indicated in the notion of parrhesia introduced above. Foucault stresses that Socrates played the role of parrhesiast vis-à-vis Alcibiades (a role into which Hamann loved to cast his friends), refusing to "flatter him" as others did and encouraging him instead to "learn to take care of himself," even though it meant "provoking Alcibiades' anger." This care of self, Foucault shows later, is then extended to mean that one must also take care of others and indeed must change one's own life. Thus the parrhesiastic relationship became essential for the concept of conversion among early Christians, as well,[20] and it is clear that Hamann is drawing on both models in his relationships. A related link in his typology is the Socratic ignorance which he posits as a prefiguration of the humility preached by Christ and then later by Paul (1 Corinthians 8:2–3): "Anyone who claims to know something does not yet have the necessary knowledge; but anyone who loves God is known by him." Just as he uses his friends' rejection to identify with the spurned Christ, Hamann puts on "the Socratic mask"[21] again and again, casting himself in the role of the prophet whose feigned ignorance leads others to self-knowledge.[22]

In his most famous letter to Kant, however, Hamann seizes upon a different aspect of Socrates' legacy to cast Kant in that role instead, namely his popularity in the eighteenth century as the patron of Enlightenment philosophy. Over the years, Hamann would refer metonymically to that philosophy using only Kant's name (and, incidentally, would use the phrase "pure reason" to refer metonymically to Kant).[23] So it is that Hamann makes this one exception to his frequent self-identification with Socrates. "If you are Socrates," he writes to Kant in 1759, "and if your friend [Berens] wishes to be Alcibiades, then you will need the voice of a genius to instruct you" (R 1:429–30; ZH 1:373). This "voice of genius" refers to Socrates' daemon, which inspires and instructs all his thoughts and actions.[24] Hamann assumes the voice of Socrates' guiding spirit, then, as a supplement to the voice of the Christian God, in these negotiations with his friends.

Hegel does not devote much attention to these classical references, perhaps considering them nothing more than an alternative way for Hamann to assert a superiority which is, at heart, Protestant piety. The ultimate conclusion which Hegel derives from the letters of this period is that Hamann's "dialectic is the religious one, which abstractly asserts his superiority over so-called earthly duties and over activity in and for existing relationships, and which confines his haphazard personality within this superiority." Yet Hegel notes that "the bond of friendship" is "unshakeable" (*HH*, 15) for Hamann, even in the face of his dispute with Kant and Berens. Hegel explains that a "disagreement" about principles, "though it can of course go quite a way, cannot disturb a friendship born of a common foundation." To this truism he attributes Hamann's "constancy in friendship" (25–26). While we may praise Hamann's loyalty here (as many commentators have), Hegel's conclusion seems to qualify the degree to which Hamann is capable of a productive earthly friendship, having isolated himself in his pious superiority. Accordingly, the letters intended to negotiate the dispute with the Berens household ultimately stopped, after Kant stopped replying to Hamann altogether and Hamann felt he was having equally little success with Berens or even Lindner. In the end, as Hegel puts it, Hamann's "pride," along with the "premises" to which he held fast, "made it impossible for any understanding to be reached" (18).

The most important consequence of this personal upheaval, however, was yet to come. Hegel reads the whole dispute as the catalyst for Hamann's authorial development and entire literary career. Once the correspondence had broken off in 1759, Hamann decided to try and influence his friends, to formulate his resistance to their requests that he join them in the light of reason, with the essay which he held to be the true beginning of his authorship, the *Socratic Memorabilia*.[25] Hegel identifies the specific impetus for this work as Hamann's need to be recognized by his friends as their teacher and prophet. But since Kant and Berens had so vehemently resisted his adoption of this pose (Berens being so disgusted by it that he refused to allow his sister to marry Hamann), Hamann was left to adopt it also toward the public. Hence the doubled dedication of the *Memorabilia*: "To the Public, or Nobody, the Notorious"; and "To the Two," or Kant and Berens. In other words, Hegel attributes the beginning of Hamann's career as a serious writer to his falling-out with his friends.[26]

Moreover, it is Hamann's understanding of friendship that shapes what he hopes to accomplish with the *Memorabilia*. The notion of friendship frames Hamann's second dedication of the *Memorabilia*, which is directed at his friends and begins with the hope that "the affection of friendship will perhaps disclose to you, my gentlemen, a little microscopic forest in these pages," "where a common reader might see nothing but mold," and ends with the assurance that "since you are both my friends, your partisan praise and your partisan rebuke will be equally welcome" (R 2:11–12; N 2:61). Not only does this dedication demonstrate that the piece which follows will be in many respects a continuation of the foregoing dispute, but it also announces, publicly, how central the idea of friendship is to all that Hamann hopes to accomplish. It is likely his friends did not respond better to the *Memorabilia* because Hamann continued here to assert a Socratic-cum-Christian superiority.[27]

After the conflict with Kant and Berens had subsided somewhat, Hamann continued to consider both men friends, as he had even in the heat of the dispute. The last letter he wrote to Kant, his final attempt to convince him before the *Socratic Memorabilia*, begins: "Dear Friend! This name is not an empty word for me, but rather a source of interrelated duties and delights" (R 1:504; ZH 1:448). Whenever he was in Königsberg, even much later in their lives, Hamann visited Kant, at his home and during Kant's renowned walks, with some frequency. The visits were not reciprocated, but Kant did extend Hamann certain kindnesses, helping to secure employment for him at a time when he sorely needed it and waiving the tuition fees when he became the teacher of Hamann's son.[28] But the relationship remained a strained one, as Hamann continued to move away from the brand of Enlightenment which Kant came to epitomize more and more, writing severe critiques of Kant's "Answer to the Question: What Is Enlightenment?"[29] and, in the *Metacritique* which receives much attention from Hegel, the *Critique of Pure Reason*.[30] But as Isaiah Berlin puts it: "Through it all, [Hamann] likes Kant; Kant is wrong-headed, hopelessly bemused by his own fantasies, but a decent old friend whose character one respects."[31] While the Hamann scholar James O'Flaherty writes that "there developed between [Kant and Hamann] an element of genuine friendship in spite of the philosophical and religious gulf which separated them,"[32] Kant's biographer Manfred Kuehn maintains that Kant was never "a close friend of Hamann and . . . usually met him because they were part of the same circle of friends."[33]

Regardless of Kant's sentiments, Hamann's constancy toward Kant (and toward Berens and Lindner, for that matter, with whom he resumed contact) is characteristic. He believes in maintaining friendships at all costs, and feels that "any break between two old friends is absolutely the most horrid thing, and a true cancer of the heart" (R 7:143; ZH 5:168). He writes to Lindner in 1761 that "no break should occur in the laws of friendship, namely those which exist in the spirit rather than in the letter, which are the sentiments of the heart and not the articles of convention" (R 3:95; ZH 2:104). Thus Morgan misses Hamann's dedication to lasting friendship as fervently as to truth itself when she claims that he "prefers the tension of the too much, even if it threatens to result in an explosive mixture between the you and I, blowing the friends further apart, beyond recuperation."[34] Friendship and truth are, for Hamann, inseparable. While he is commenting on altogether different thinkers and texts (albeit mainly of the same era), Fenves aptly summarizes Hamann's sentiments here, namely that friends "must say what they deem to be true not for the sake of the truth but for the sake of friendship . . . without reserve and without bounds," and this "for the sake of *possible* friendships or, in other words, friendships to come—not for the sake of certain friendships that they are confidant [*sic*] they have secured."[35]

What is more, Hamann expects to experience the same loyalty from his friends. In 1776, for example, after his letters to Reichardt are met only with a long silence, Hamann writes that that silence has hurt him deeply, and asks Reichardt to reply in friendship. "It is difficult for me," he admits, "to leave unrebuked sins against the spirit of friendship" (R 5:195; ZH 3:272). Again Hamann assumes the role of his friend's rebuker, but it is the maintenance of a valued friendship which is at stake. This piously pedagogical streak toward his friends, like his utter devotion to them, will continue to surface throughout Hamann's life, but no relationship will be quite as thoroughly and consequentially affected by it as the ones which led to the *Socratic Memorabilia*.

A New "Alcibiades": Herder

In commenting on the "excitability" which characterized Hamann's "friend-addiction" (*das Freundessüchtige*), the nineteenth-century literary historian G. G. Gervinus notes that as "the new Socrates," Hamann "was always longing for an Alcibiadean friend" who would grant him "as much honor and adulation . . . as he demanded."[36] For a long and significant period, that friend was Johann Gottfried Herder, who was studying in Königsberg when he met Hamann and their legendary friendship began.[37] Nadler suggests that Herder represented, at the beginning of the friendship, "a pupil whom Hamann could raise for himself into the intellectual companion he had been missing," and then later nothing less than a "disciple."[38] Herder was fourteen years younger than Hamann, which surely facilitated the role Hamann desired. Hamann's early letters to Herder are full of advice and guidance, both personal and professional, and Nadler indicates that Herder, in turn, took on the role of "imprudent Alcibiades at the breast of Socrates."[39]

The relationship blossomed into "one of the exemplary, most intel-

lectually fruitful and perhaps greatest friendships of the eighteenth century," and the correspondence it yielded became "one of the most precious attestations of personality and of humanity" at that time.[40] This
could only have been the case because Herder did not resist the authori-
tative pose which Hamann adopted, at least not in the manner Kant and
Berens had. To be sure, Hamann had learned to present himself in this
pose in a more palatable way, but the situation was also aided by the fact
that Herder had more insight into and sympathy for Hamann's way of
thinking than any of his previous friends had.

But the seeds of dissension were always there in the friendship.
Hamann complains frequently that Herder does not respond to his letters
quickly or often enough. He takes issue with much of the work which
Herder sends him while it is in progress, and Herder does not always accept the criticism without defending himself. While Hegel remarks upon
the "continuous" "tone of intimate friendship" between the two, he also
notes that it often waxes "quite stilted or even satirical" (*HH,* 26), that
their communications lose "more and more of their vitality of sentiment,"
until finally they fall "into the boredom of pious lamentation." In this regard Hegel quotes a 1787 letter from Hamann to Herder: "For some years
now, my dull, feeble correspondence must have been to you a true mirror
of my sad situation" (45). Herder, Hegel tells us, responds more or less
in kind.

A similarly "stilted" and "satirical" tone distinguishes Hamann's
writings about Herder (*Herderschriften*). The problem that Herder's
prizewinning essay on the origin of language and Hamann's responses to
it caused for the friendship seems to have stemmed from the lack of mutual understanding conveyed in all these pages. Hamann writes to
Herder in June of 1772 that many of his friends from Courland and Livonia (where he had lived while working as a tutor) "no longer understand
me at all, and this is a bad omen for our friendship" (R 5:6; ZH 3:8). But
just a few months later the same omen would present itself between these
two friends, as Hamann was finishing his *Knight of the Rose-Cross* and *Philological Ideas and Doubts,* both of them responses to Herder's now-famous
essay, and both unflattering in a number of respects. Upon reading the
former, along with the reviews of the prize essay which Hamann had written for periodicals, Herder writes to him: "I do not understand everything, nor do I know how you have written all that . . . , as your manner
of thinking has never been fully accessible to me, nor has it been my understanding. So I accept all [these] pieces as from the blind and golden
age of Saturn; I understand as much as I can understand, and I make use
of as much as I can use." Herder's real issue, however, goes beyond an in-
nocent lack of understanding; he does not believe that Hamann has

made clear the significant difference between the two men on the problem of language: "But it is still incomprehensible to me, how . . . your [conception of the] faculty of speech diverges from mine" (R 5:7–8; ZH 3:10). In his very next letter (R 5:15–19; ZH 3:15–18), Hamann informs Herder of his next response (*Philological Ideas and Doubts*), then in press, in which Hamann calls into question the entire premise of Herder's essay, even the honesty of its intentions. It must have put a further strain on their friendship when Herder asked Hamann not to publish it. Hamann complied, and to be sure, all the letters from this time are filled with reassurances from both parties of enduring affection and loyalty. But the persistent lack of understanding and satisfactory explanation between the two men does seem to have changed the nature of their friendship going forward. The best proof of this change is found in the eventual decline in their correspondence, which coincided with the new friendship that became the centerpiece of Hamann's life.

"Bruder Jonathan": Jacobi

Upon befriending the philosopher Friedrich Heinrich Jacobi, Hamann gave him the nickname "Jonathan" to evoke the biblical friendship between David and Jonathan (2 Samuel 1:26: "My brother Jonathan, greatly beloved were you to me; your love to me was wonderful, passing the love of women.")[41] The climax of Hamann's prolific correspondence with Jacobi, which sometimes included the exchange of up to eight letters per month, came in 1786. Hamann wrote almost forty letters to Jacobi that year; only four were sent to Herder.[42] If the Hamann-Herder correspondence was one of "constancy and intellectual depth," then that between Hamann and Jacobi took on a "closeness and psychic warmth." If Herder had been Hamann's pupil and disciple, then Jacobi became the "mature man" alongside Hamann, even if the tone of their letters did often include a "boyish humor" and "enthusiastic tenderness"[43] which Hegel characterizes as "most intimate and reckless" (*HH*, 6). Such intimacy—Jacobi was the only correspondent with whom Hamann used the informal *du* address—was possible, we can assume, because of the "trust" Hegel observes between the two: "In each other's presence, Jacobi was to find Hamann's soul . . . and to recognize and learn to understand therein the resolution of all misunderstandings, the explanation of the riddle of spirit" (50).

But this friendship, too, entered a period of strained difficulty. Nadler calls it a mood of "helpless kindness" and suggests that it stemmed from this fundamental difference: that Jacobi, "the philosopher of the heart, sought God with his emotions and envied Hamann's faith," whereas Hamann, who "believed without himself really knowing with which of his organs," could not help Jacobi in this matter.[44] But Hegel seems to attribute any distance or resentment on Jacobi's part to Hamann's "utterly disapproving explosions" about Jacobi's work, for "certainly nothing more sensitive could have happened to [Jacobi]" (*HH*, 50). These "explosions" arose from Hamann's basic rejection of Jacobi's differentiation between idealism and realism.[45] This disapproval is characteristic of Hamann. As Hegel explains at length, Hamann's chief problem with Mendelssohn and with the late Kant was their shared practice of dividing strictly into categories things which Hamann fervently believed were and must remain united in nature.[46] Jacobi was forced to admit that he did not understand Hamann's beloved *principium coincidentiae* in this regard.[47] Hamann, however, diagnosed his friend's problem as a lack of the *self*-understanding that was, for him, so important not only to the development of one's philosophy, but also to friendship itself. "You do not understand yourself," he writes to Jacobi, "and you are too overhasty to make yourself understood by others, and to impart your sickly philosophy to others out of a principle of goodwill" (ZH 7:168).

While the two men remained extremely fond of each other up until Hamann's death, it does seem, given his criticisms of Jacobi's thought and Jacobi's responses to them, that the problems in this friendship, too, trace back to the lack of a certain understanding, both of oneself and of each other. And this, Hegel tells us, is exactly what Jacobi had hoped to find in Hamann: "the resolution of all misunderstandings." Instead, having finally met Hamann in person after all their exchange of letters, Jacobi is ultimately left to admit to Johann Kaspar Lavater, a mutual friend, that he has "not been able to fathom" Hamann's "art of living and being happy." This, Hegel posits, "is not to be called a misunderstanding, but rather a lack of understanding; [Jacobi] is not made confused by [Hamann's] presence, but rather remains confused." It seems the disappointment was mutual; after staying awhile in Jacobi's house, Hamann left quite "suddenly" and even stealthily (*HH*, 52). We may be reminded of Hamann's insistence upon the bond between two friends "even if they feel compelled to live according to different schemata," but it seems that this condition ultimately prohibited a deeper connection between Hamann and even his most intimate friend, who still could not claim to understand him in the end.

In the friendships examined thus far, we have seen Hamann living in mostly pleasant fraternity with a number of the eighteenth century's most illustrious men of letters. But we have also observed a clear pattern in these epoch-making friendships with Kant, Herder, and then Jacobi. In the early going, a spark of intellectual attraction ignites sentiments which are (often quite literally) reminiscent of a love affair, and friendship is seen as a marvelous gift from God which allows friends to identify with one another. But at some point a dispute arises with regard to one's philosophical stance, one's mode of being and of thinking. As Hegel puts it, Hamann "becomes so agitated precisely by the writings of his best friends that he attacks them in essays intended for publication, charged with his usual manner of passionate virulence and mischief, which are themselves not without a component which can be perceived as bitter scorn, and can be quite insulting" (*HH*, 26).[48] In the cases of Herder and Jacobi, this criticism may seem all the more unfathomable given the extent to which these men are drawing on Hamann in the development of their own ideas. At any rate, while this turn of events does not lead to a complete dissolution of a friendship far too important simply to fall away, it does place the strain of disillusionment onto people who no longer find it possible to understand each other in a way that leads to mutual identification, let alone spiritual betterment. This disillusionment leads Hamann repeatedly to seek out a new connection which offers greater fulfillment, again in the manner that a disappointed lover might seek out a new partner, such that the cycle repeats.

In order to ask whether Hamann ever found such a fulfilling connection, we must examine some later friendships that are quite different from those just synthesized. This synthesis began with an allusion to Hamann's fraternity among fellow *men* of letters, but he also enjoyed friendships with a number of women. Hamann writes numerous times of his friends Sophie Marianne Courtan (née Toussaint, Hartknoch's sister-in-law) and Karoline Stolz, who had come from Courland and seemed also to have some connection to Lavater. Hamann enjoyed a long friendship with the Baroness Bondelli, whom he had once tutored in English, and who eventually took in and educated Hamann's daughters.[49] He corresponded not only with J. G. Herder but also with Herder's wife, Caroline. "Recommend me to your dear husband," he writes to her in 1779, "to whom I have never really said how much you deserve to be his First and Only Friend [*Freundin*]; for truth and friendship have always been the highest objects in my economy, which one must proliferate not for the present moment but for the last moments of life" (R 6:74; ZH 4:60). He also writes to Caroline about the link he perceives between friendship and marriage, in a way that explains the parallel we observe in him between friendships and romantic relationships: "In friendship, as in marriage, the blame often lies with both parties. If each would recognize his failings, each would be more able to carry the burden of the other, to take the cross upon himself which is inevitable" (R 7:209; ZH 5:354).[50] These sentiments notwithstanding, it must be said that Hamann's relationship with his own common-law wife, Anna Regina Schumacher, does not seem to have enjoyed this status of "friendship," as Hegel's essay makes clear.[51]

Still, Nadler claims that "Hamann naturally understood how to have women as friends."[52] A qualifying elucidation of what this might mean for Nadler, or have meant for Hamann, is found in a late letter to Jacobi which Hegel quotes, a letter Hamann wrote after living for a time in the home of Jacobi and his two sisters. He accuses Jacobi of burdening these sisters, "which nature made softer and tamer, with the hard yoke" of a "friendship" far too "masculine." What is meant by this, we can infer, is that Jacobi has included his sisters in the philosophical discussions between himself and Hamann, for Hamann notes that "these two *Amazons* made it a point to deprive me, poor old man, of the honor of my whole philosophy, of all of your favorable judgments thereof, and to bring us both into such embarrassment that we would seem ridiculous to each other and even to ourselves, like a couple of *philosophical ghosts*" (*HH*, 52). This sheds more light on the disillusionment that accompanied the first actual meeting between Hamann and Jacobi, following the relative ecstasy of their long correspondence, as Hamann implies it was partially Jacobi's sisters who led the two into disagreement or perhaps misunderstanding. Hamann's attempt to contain the "soft," "tame" sisters in his scolding of Jacobi fails, as they emerge instead as the threatening "Amazons" who wield the considerable power to thwart the progress of philosophical understanding between the two male friends. Hegel interprets this as another instance of Hamann's inability to make himself understood, this time, crucially, "among clever ladies (with whom one could not get by with the blustering and crudities with which [Hamann] served himself)." The added onus placed on Hamann's thought by this supposedly uniquely feminine demand that it "step out of its nebulousness to the clarity of thought or sentiment" rendered his "philosophizing" mere "feelings of affliction and fear" (52). Hamann's best response to this threat, it seems, was to keep discussions of this nature away from such women.

"The Christian Aspasia": Princess Gallitzin

Hamann did find, toward the end of his life, a woman friend with whom he could share at least parts of his "philosophizing." This was Princess Adelheid Amalia von Gallitzin, the well-known wife of a prominent Russian diplomat. Having spurned religion and the Bible earlier in her life, she was now, in the 1780s, a devout woman who became a great admirer of Hamann's—particularly of his connection between Greek philosophy and Christianity—after reading the *Socratic Memorabilia*. He met her personally while living with the Buchholtz family near Münster, where Gallitzin had assembled quite a circle around her in the interest of educating herself and her children. This circle included the educational reformers Franz von Fürstenberg and Bernhard Heinrich Overberg, as well as the poet Count Leopold Stolberg[53] and the Dutch philosopher Frans Hemsterhuis.[54] In the company of these new friends, Hamann went from borrowing Hemsterhuis's nickname for the princess, "Diotima" (Hemsterhuis had dedicated his 1785 "Lettre de Dioclès à Diotime sur l'athéisme" to her) to assigning his own, calling her in his late letters "the Christian Aspasia" (R 7:423; ZH 7:495), in reference to the exceptional woman of antiquity characterized by her unusual intellect and public influence. The references to the princess as an Aspasia and as the "Goethe of her gender" (R 7:362; ZH 7:248) set her apart from the sort of woman who posed a threat to Hamann's thought, as both nicknames distance her from the rest of her sex and imply a more facile (because more masculine and thus less questioning) access to this kind of philosophy.

The other comfort Hamann was able to feel among Gallitzin's circle was his identity as a Christian above all other things. Writing about this late-eighteenth-century group, Karlfried Gründer notes that "the religious was above all an element and a means of the process of self-formation and education," which depended upon "a model of Christian virtue which blended both Catholic piety, in the form especially of the French pastoral literature of the seventeenth century, and the Protestant Pietism of the late eighteenth century."[55] Among these new friends, then, Hamann found a place where friendly rebuke and preaching were more welcome, such that he became the princess's "spiritual leader and fatherly minister, even intercessory saint."[56] In fact, an apt summary of Hamann's time with Gallitzin and her friends is found, remarkably, in the Chrysostom passage he had quoted to his brother so many years before. These people truly seemed to be "friends to the glory of God" who tried to keep each other's "souls in order," to "admonish" and "support" each other, to bring each other to God. In their company, Hamann felt himself "in the bosom of friends cast from the same mold, who fit like other halves to my ideals of the soul." He even compares his experience among them to "a foretaste of heaven on earth" (R 7:409; ZH 7:406). These reflections are likely colored by the illness and impending death which defined Hamann's time in Münster. Gallitzin was at his side when he died (R 7:432), and he was buried in her garden. Her papers give the fullest account of the last year of Hamann's life, and his final letters to friends and family are full of her praises.

And still there are signs of deep dissatisfaction, signs that Hamann has not found the intimate connection he had sought so often and for so long. To be sure, this dissatisfaction does not develop along the same lines we have observed, in the wake of a critical response to a friend's philosophy or publications, or a friend's refusal to play the role of disciple. But the origin of this dissatisfaction does still seem to be a basic lack of understanding. This is something Hegel discusses extensively, and in an especially Hegelian manner, on account of which we must quote him at length here.

> As much as reciprocal respect and love and equality in the reason of opinions surrounded this fine circle, it lay nonetheless in the manner and constitution of friendship itself that this circle also fell, if not into resentment, then at least into mutual incomprehensibility, and labored about therein. And incomprehensibility is perhaps worse than resentment, in that incomprehensibility is connected to and torments with the misunderstanding of oneself, whereas resentment may only be directed at others. . . . If we seek out the reason that this joy, in which such excellent individuals found themselves together, proceeded into the unexpected consequence that they ended up nonetheless in dissatisfaction, it probably lies in the contradiction [*in dem Widerspruche*] in which they believed and took themselves and each other to be. If dispositions, thoughts, ideas, interests, principles, beliefs, and sentiments are communicable among humans, then in the view of this circle, the naked, concentrated intensity of mind and faith lay *outside of* and *behind* this concreteness of individuality. This deepest and simplest thing alone was to bear absolute value and was to be found, known, and enjoyed only through the living presence of a confident intimacy which gave itself completely and held nothing back. Those who fixed such separation in their minds and tied to it their concept of beauty and even magnificence of the soul cannot satisfy each other with thoughts and deeds, with the objectivity of disposition, faith, sentiments. But the inside is only revealed, shown, communicated in that manner of sentiments, ideas, thoughts, deeds, etc. Now since in such communicating the differences and particularities of viewpoints come forth into ambiguity—for the entire situation is ambiguity itself—just as the appearance as such does not correspond to that inwardness so sought after, so demanded, so seemingly *unutterable,* and the soul [*Psyche*] itself does not give itself to

understanding as such, the result is then *indéfinissable*, an incomprehensibility and unsatisfied longing, a mood in which people, without really being able to say why, find themselves separated and estranged from each other, instead of having found each other, as they believed. (*HH,* 47–48)

Hegel's analysis falls in line with Hamann's life philosophy inasmuch as it is the principle of understanding upon which friendship relies, and without which it necessarily suffers, regardless of the mutual affection and admiration it might enjoy. But at the beginning and the end of this passage, Hegel is clearly attributing a certain lack of understanding, and thus of communication, to "the manner and constitution of friendship itself." Hamann, on the other hand, never seems to have accepted this as a truism, even after being disappointed by it time after time. Instead, Hamann blames this lack of understanding again and again on his individual friends, wavering between the criticism that they did not understand him and that they did not understand themselves. Hegel's study of these relationships, in contrast, leads him to a more nuanced distinction between "incomprehensibility" and "resentment," one he clearly considers to be a characteristic of friendship globally, not just of the Münster circle.

Hegel's thoughts on that particular circle are found in the middle of the passage. What *is* unique to people of this sort, he says, is the particular way they choose to dwell in a fundamental contradiction, which is as follows. On one side of the problem is the fact that we only have "dispositions, thoughts, ideas, interests, principles, beliefs, and sentiments" with which to communicate our individualities to each other. On this point, Hegel, Hamann, and the Münster circle seem to be largely in agreement. But on the other side of the problem is an assumption held by the Münster group which Hegel does not share, namely that what is real, deep, and true is inherently external to the individuality we are capable of communicating, and that one can only hope to access this deeper reality on any significant level via intimacy with other like-minded people. But how can we hope to achieve such intimacy if we know from the outset that our thoughts and ideas cannot communicate on any level that corresponds to that which we hold to be most true, to our absolute? Here Hegel shows that for the Münster circle and others like them, the problem goes beyond an inevitable contradiction, and lies even more so in a strict separation which he believes is artificial and thus foolishly espoused. How strange that Hegel should be able to accuse the mature Hamann, the champion of the *principium coincidentiae,* of laboring under a false separation. Yet this is a key component of the mutual incomprehensibilty among Hamann and his friends, despite their apparent similarities.

Hegel sheds more light on the distinction between the Münster circle and everyone else who must grapple with the aporias of human interaction in his reference to "beauty and even magnificence of the soul." The cult of the beautiful soul [*schöne Seele*] was an essential element of spirituality in Germany in the eighteenth and early nineteenth centuries. According to its ideal, inner beauty is sought and found via the kinship of the heart which is an intensely personal Christianity. This beauty inspires a virtuous life lived in friendship and affection, possible only when one lives in perpetual examination of the soul. This is the very conception of friendship that Hegel implies bound the Münster circle together. But Hegel criticizes the subjective indulgence of this ideal more clearly in the *Phenomenology of Mind* than in the Hamann piece. He does so in its discussion of conscience (*Gewissen*), which in the case of the beautiful soul is cut off from society in its extreme turn inward. This turn represents a rejection of both objectivity and societal duty, and allows for a lapse into mysticism despite intentions toward goodness. Thus the beautiful soul, in Hegel's words, "does not possess the strength to relinquish the self-absorbed uncommunicative knowledge of itself," "cannot succeed in seeing the unity of its self in another life," and "cannot reach objective existence." Moreover, the beautiful soul "has no concrete reality," but lingers instead "in the contradiction [*in dem Widerspruche*] between its pure self and the necessity felt by this self to externalize itself and turn into something actual." This must be the same *contradiction* to which Hegel refers in the long passage on Hamann in Münster cited above, the one which makes these friends incommunicable to themselves and to each other. Hegel does credit the beautiful soul with being at least "conscious of this contradiction in its unreconciled immediacy," but this consciousness simply means that the beautiful soul becomes "unhinged, disordered, and runs to madness, wastes itself in yearning, and pines away in consumption."[57]

These maxims from the *Phenomenology* elucidate Hegel's conviction that, for the Münster circle, adherence (even if not overly dogmatic) to the notion of the beautiful soul, to the absolute held in suspension at its center, yields a lack of faith in the ability of traditional communication to satisfy their longing. This could not have been, Hegel argues, anything other than an utterly isolating and isolated position. Hamann had always isolated himself in the resolute insistence that no one understood him; this was, he believed, the source of so many problems in his friendships. His only consolation, Hegel tells us, was the reminder that "*God* understands me" (*HH,* 45). But Hegel's essay together with his ruminations from the *Phenomenology* demonstrate that this consolation too remained problematic, because it allowed Hamann to withdraw from his friends and into himself, into the piety which had always alienated him and now did so even further.

Before concluding the matter, we must introduce one more text in which Hegel reflects generally on friendship, again because of the undeniable connection to the sentiments expressed in the Hamann essay. In the *Lectures on the Philosophy of Religion* delivered the year before the Hamann piece appeared, Hegel says: "Ethical life, love, means precisely the giving up of particularity, of particular personality, and its extension to universality—so, too, with friendship. In friendship and love I give up my abstract personality and thereby win it back as concrete. The truth of personality is found precisely in winning it back through this immersion, this being immersed in the other."[58] This elucidates much of the critique Hegel has levied at Hamann throughout the review, as Hegel's recounting of the conflicts with the Berens family, with Kant, and with others has been colored by his disapproval of Hamann's refusal to sacrifice, even momentarily, his absolute "particularity." Had Hamann even attempted this as an exercise in "immersion" into the other, the *Lectures* seem to argue, he would likely have arrived at an individuality far more "concrete" and "true" than the isolated idiosyncrasy in which he languished until the very end of his "besieged life" (*HH*, 53). Particularly in his final months, among his Münster friends, Hamann could not hope to see his personality undergo this purification, because he and his friends had not first accessed their own respective individualities with the depth required for them then to immerse these individualities into each other and "win them back." They could not have done so because their individualities were, as Hegel establishes in the long passage quoted above, too far removed from their "concentrated intensity of mind and faith," from their "absolute."

Hegel's own understanding of friendship, as expressed both in the *Lectures* and in his Hamann review, are, John McCumber points out, based on the principle of enlarged thought which Kant puts forth in the *Critique of Judgment*. In McCumber's paraphrase, enlarged thought means that "we undertake to test the results of our judgment against the opinions of others . . . , ready to learn from them and revise our views if need be."[59] If Hegel laments again and again the fact that Hamann was loathe "to submit his thought to others in this way," it is because the consequences of such stubbornness went beyond a personal decision which affected a small circle of people.[60] Friendship was perceived as so much more than that in the eighteenth and early nineteenth centuries. It was a "determinative socio-ethical category" which combined "classical and Christian moral doctrine" with "thought about natural law, behavioral theory, social hygiene, and politics,"[61] and was expected to contribute "not so much" to "everyday life" as to "the founding of society, the legal order, and the sphere of political action."[62] The philosophy of Kant and Hegel is extremely Aristotelian in this sense, evoking the latter's claim that friendship "seems too to hold states together," since "concord seems to be something like friendship."[63] Thus, when Hamann refused to enlarge his thought, to weigh his judgments against those of his friends, he was spurning, in Hegel's view, not only his friends, but also a key foundation of the social and legal order. This, then, is the true impetus for all Hegel's critique of Hamann's behavior in his friendships, and the reason this often quite personal critique cannot be separated from that of Hamann as a thinker and writer.

The foregoing is not to imply that Hegel gives Hamann no credit whatsoever for gleaning from his friendships some benefit for his societal character. While acknowledging the "probability that [Hamann] would follow the path of hypocrisy," as we saw in the discussion of his desire to be the pedagogue who leads his friends to self-knowledge, Hegel ultimately notes that Hamann "was saved from [this probability] by the strong and fresh root of friendship in his mind, by the ingenious vitality of his spirit and his nobler temperament." This was the case because the "root of friendship did not allow [Hamann] to be dishonest with himself or with his friends, nor to spurn the principle of worldly judiciousness" (*HH*, 28). To be sure, by the end of his life, friendship had performed a number of different services in Hamann's life, remarkably in line with Aristotle's praise of the virtue which "helps the young . . . to keep from error" (Kant, Berens, Lindner), "aids older people by ministering to their needs and supplementing the activities that are failing from weakness" (the Münster circle), and "stimulates" people in the time in between "to noble actions . . . , for with friends men are more able both to think and to act" (Herder, Jacobi).[64]

In many respects, then, we see in Hegel a more nuanced understanding of the nature of friendship than is present in many of Hamann's resolute convictions. Hegel grasps the dialectic between nobility and hypocrisy, between intimacy and distance, between community and individuality, in a way that Hamann often does not, as evidenced by Hamann's strict pronouncements to and censures of his friends. These sentiments, Hegel's analysis suggests, were never subjected to the kind of inner development which might have turned them into socially fruitful principles of interaction. This notion of development, or the lack thereof, is central to Hegel's critique of Hamann as a writer and a person, and it is thoroughly grounded in Hegel's own assumptions and beliefs. In the passage in which Hegel most frequently refers to this kind of developing (*Entfalten*), he adopts a metaphor Hamann had chosen and chastises him for contenting himself with a "balled fist," rather than "go[ing] to the effort" of "un-clench[ing]" his thought (and his own personality) "into an *open hand.*" As we noted in the previous essay, this metaphor also introduces the central difference between Hamann's and Hegel's conceptions of God. For Hamann, God is at the same time both the absolute ground of all language and thus all knowledge and also, through Christ, an intimate friend. For Hegel, God is at the same time both a "balled core of truth" and also the very force which develops or unfolds—the German word *ent-falten* implies both—that truth "into a system of nature, into a system of the state, of justice and morality, into a system of world history, into an open hand with fingers outstretched." This divine unfolding, Hegel continues, makes "the human spirit" what it is, namely "not merely an abstruse intelligence, a dull, concentrated weaving in itself, not merely a feeling and practicing" (read: Hamann), "but rather a developed system of intelligent organization whose formal peak is thought." Consequently, it is our duty as humans, Hegel concludes, "to enter into this unfolding by way of reflection *on* it" (*HH,* 39) and in this way to develop our own personalities in an analogous manner. Thus, the ultimate failing which Hegel cannot excuse in Hamann, which tempers his entire review, is that Hamann did not "unfold" himself into this development, as his devotion to increased knowledge of God and of self, frequently acquired via the ideal of friendship, would seem to have demanded.

The Writings of Hamann

By G. W. F. Hegel

First Article

The public is most greatly indebted to the esteemed editor for the fact that he now, through his promotion and perseverance, delivers into our hands the writings of *Hamann,* previously accessible in their entirety only to a few and with great difficulty, and after so many prospects of their complete reprinting had fallen through. Hamann himself did not give satisfaction (R 1:x, prologue) to various invitations to organize a collection of his writings. Only a few possessed a complete collection of them; *Goethe* (*From My Life,* book 12) had had the idea to attend to the editing and publication of Hamann's works, but did not carry it out.[1] *Jacobi,* who made serious arrangements toward such an undertaking, was not granted that good fortune. A younger friend of Hamann, Real Privy Superior Government Councilor Herr L. *Nicolovius* in Berlin,[2] declined the task and instead called upon our editor, an intimate friend of Jacobi's in the later part of Jacobi's life, whom Jacobi had chosen to assist him with the publication. Thus our editor carried out the bequest of his dear, esteemed friend and satisfied the wishes of the public, exceptionally favored at the same time by the additional fortune (R 1:xii) of having received from friends or heirs of Hamann a large number of letters to be printed, including some in a succession spanning several years, so that he was able to furnish this edition with them, which means that only a few circumstances or complications of Hamann's life will remain about which we have not been informed. To that which is brought together in this collection, we should add the third section of the fourth volume of *Jacobi's* works, in which is found the extremely interesting correspondence between Hamann and this intimate friend, but whose publisher did not permit a new printing of this correspondence to be made for the present collection.[3] For a number of years we have looked forward, in vain, to the promised *eighth* volume of this edition, which shall contain commentaries, in part by Hamann himself, perhaps supplements from letters, and an index; since its appearance can apparently be expected to be delayed for a considerable time, we shall not postpone any longer this long intended review, as desirable as it would have been to have the promised commentaries already in hand.[4] One feels the dire need for these commentaries when reading Hamann's works; but the hope of receiving elucidation from the promised volume is in any case greatly diminished when one reads, on page x of the prologue, that it was the impossibility, acknowledged by Hamann himself, of elucidating all which is dark in his writings, that prevented him from organizing their publication. *Jacobi* as well had been impeded in this task by the formidability of this demand, and the current editor says on page xiii that the commentaries which are to follow in the eighth volume will satisfy only a very moderate expectation, and that the chronological order of the writings, primarily the many letters regarding Hamann's authorship, must provide the principal facilitation of understanding. In addition, one soon learns that mysteriousness itself belongs to the characteristic temperament of Hamann's writing and individuality, and constitutes an essential current thereof. The primary obscurity, however, which lay over Hamann generally, has already disappeared now that his writings are before us. The *Allgemeine Deutsche Bibliothek* [*Public German Library*][5] had of course concerned itself much with him, but not in such a manner as to provide public recognition and access. *Herder,* on the other hand, and especially *Jacobi* (as witnessed in *Goethe's* singular comment, cited on page x of the prologue, which however must be qualified by Goethe's more elaborate and thorough appraisal of Hamann [loc. cit.])[6] speak of him in such a manner that they seemed to invoke him as one who should have come, one in full possession of the mysteries in whose reflection their own revelations merely played, just as the members of Freemason lodges are to be directed primarily to higher authorities located at the center of all the depths of the secrets of God and of nature. Thus, a nimbus had enshrouded the *Magus from the North*—this had become a sort of title for Hamann.[7] Accordingly, he himself had spoken everywhere in his writing only fragmentarily and as a sibyl, and the only writings which one could procure inspired curiosity about the others, in which one might hope to find elucidation. Through this edition of his works which now lies before us, we are able to see who Hamann was, what his wisdom and knowledge were.

To begin by considering the general situation in which Hamann emerges, he belongs to that time in which the *thinking* spirit in Germany, whose independence had arisen at first in scholarly philosophy, began now to spread [*sich ergehen*] in reality, and to lay claim to those things within it which were considered solid and true, and in which the entire domain of reality began to vindicate itself. It is characteristic of the German progress of the spirit toward its own freedom that thought found in *Wolffian philosophy* a methodical, sober form; once understanding, dealing now also with the other sciences, especially mathematics, had, in this form, penetrated general instruction and scientific culture, it now began to emerge from the academy and from its pedagogical form and to address in its foundations, in a popular way, every interest of spirit, the positive principles of the church, of the state, and of right. As much as this application of understanding lacked any spirituality, its content lacked just as much native originality. One cannot hope to conceal that this enlightening consisted solely in establishing now in Germany the principles of deism, religious tolerance, and morality which *Rousseau* and *Voltaire* had raised to the general way of thinking among the upper classes in and beyond France. While Voltaire lingered for some time in Berlin at the court of Frederick II, and many other reigning German princes (perhaps the majority) counted it as an honor to be in acquaintance, contact, or correspondence with Voltaire or his friends, the distribution of their principles went out from Berlin into the sphere of the middle classes, including the clergy, among whom the German Enlightenment counted its most active and effective collaborators, while the struggle in France was directed primarily against the clergy. There was then the further difference between the two countries that this uprising or rebellion of thought in France was embraced by everything which possessed genius, spirit, talent, nobleness, and this new manner of truth appeared with the radiance of all talents and with the vigor of a naive, spirited, energetic common sense [*gesunden Menschenverstandes*]. In Germany, on the other hand, that great impulse was divided into two different dispositions. On the one hand the business of the Enlightenment was pursued with dry understanding, with principles of bald utility, with insipidity of spirit and knowledge, paltry or ordinary passions, and, where it was most respectable, with some (albeit sober) warmth of feeling, and stood in malevolent, harassing, jeering opposition to everything which unfolded from genius, talent, or purity of spirit and mind. *Berlin* was the center of this enlightening, where Nicolai, Mendelssohn, Teller, Spalding, Zöllner, etc., were active in their writings, as well as the collective person, the *Allgemeine Deutsche Bibliothek,* in a uniform sense, though with a different sentiment; Eberhard, Steinbart, Jerusalem, etc., can be counted as neighbors in this center.[8] Located in the periphery around it was that which blossomed in genius, spirit, and depth of reason, and which was attacked and disparaged by that center in the most spiteful manner. Toward the northeast, in Königsberg, we have *Kant, Hippel, Hamann;* toward the south in Weimar and Jena *Herder, Wieland, Goethe,* later *Schiller, Fichte, Schelling,* among others; further toward the west *Jacobi* with his friends; *Lessing,* who had long been indifferent toward the goings-on in Berlin, lived in the depths of scholarship, in wholly other depths of spirit than his friends (who believed themselves to be on intimate terms with him) surmised. Hippel, for example, was the only one among the above-mentioned great men of German literature who was not exposed to the invectives of that center. Although both sides came together in the interest of freedom of spirit, the former enlightening, as a dry understanding of the finite, persecuted hatefully the feeling or consciousness of the infinite which was located on the side of the latter [enlightening], whose depth was in poetry as well as in thinking reason. From the activity of the former there remains *their work* [*das Werk*], from the latter, however, *the works* [*die Werke*], as well.

If those who had fallen under the power of the business of the Enlightenment—because formal abstractions and some general feelings of religion, humanity, and legality constituted their intellectual peaks—could only be distinguished by unimportant peculiarities, then the latter periphery was a wreath of original individualities. Among them, *Hamann* is not only also original, but, what is more, *an* Original [*ein Original*],[9] in that he persisted in a concentration of his deep particularity, which proved incapable not only of any form of universality, but also of the expansion of thinking reason as a matter of taste.[10]

Hamann stands over against the Berlin Enlightenment above all by virtue of the profoundness of his Christian orthodoxy, but such that his way of thinking is not adherence to the wooden, orthodox theology of his time; his spirit retains the highest freedom, in which nothing remains a positive, but rather is subjectivized into the spiritual present and into one's own possession. With his two friends in Königsberg, Kant and Hippel, whom he esteems and with whom he has contact, he shares a relationship of general confidence, but not of solidarity of interests. He is further differentiated from that former Enlightenment not only by content, but also on the same grounds that separated him from *Kant*, namely because the need for thinking reason remained to him foreign and misunderstood. In this respect he is closer to *Hippel*, in that he can extend his inner meaning toward the expansion of neither knowledge nor poetry, but is only capable of humorous, flashing, desultory expression. But this humor is without richness and diversity of sentiment, and completely devoid of all impulse or attempt at form; he remains limitedly subjective. He has the most in common with that friend with whom his relationship is shown in his correspondence to be most intimate and reckless, with *Jacobi*, who was capable of writing only letters and, like Hamann, no book. However, Jacobi's letters are in themselves clear; they point toward thoughts which come to a certain development, execution, and a certain progress, so that the letters become a coherent sequence and a sort of book. The French have a saying: *Le stile c'est l'homme même;* Hamann's writings do not so much *have* a particular style as they *are* style, through and through. In everything which came from Hamann's quill, his personality is so extremely intrusive and absolutely preponderant that the reader is referred at every point more so to it than to that which might be interpreted as content. In the products which are passed off as writings and are said to treat of some subject matter, one notices immediately the incomprehensible eccentricity of their author. These products are in fact a tiresome riddle, and one realizes that its solution is the individuality of the author; but this solution is not explained in the writings themselves. It is primarily this insight which is now elucidated for us in this collection, through the publication of two previously unprinted essays by Hamann: one is the autobiography he composed in 1758 and 1759, which only extends to this point in time, and thus only incorporates the beginning of his life, but also the most important turning point in his development; the other, composed at the end of his life, sought to disclose the entire intention of his authorship (R 7:vii, preface) and give an overview of it. The copious, previously unprinted correspondence completes the materials which clarify his character. We must begin from this autobiography which, as the principal novelty of this edition, deserves a more thorough review.

It is found in the first volume, pages 149–242, and is titled *Thoughts About My Life,* Psalm 94:19 (the beginning), written in *London,* dated April 21, 1758.[11] Hamann's disposition here is also expressed in the staid and well-stylized—and thus better written than most of his later writings—opening of another essay, *Biblical Meditations of a Christian,* also written in *London,* dated March 19, Palm Sunday 1758:

> I began today, with God, to read the Holy Scriptures for the second time. As my circumstances impose upon me the greatest solitude, in which I sit like a sparrow on the rooftop and watch, I find in the company of my books, in the activity and exercise which they give to my thoughts, an antidote to the bitterness of many sad meditations on my past foolishness, about the misuse of the beneficence and circumstances with which Providence has so mercifully chosen to distinguish me. . . . The sciences and those friends of my reason seem to test my patience, like Job's, more than they comfort me, and to cause the wounds of my experience to bleed more than they ease their pain. Nature put into all bodies a salt which the chemists know how to extract, and Providence (so it seems) put into all adversities an original moral element which we are to release and separate out, which we can apply with great usefulness as an aid against the diseases of our nature and the evils of our mind. If we fail to see God in the sunlight, in the pillar of cloud, then his presence appears to us by night in the pillar of fire more visibly and more emphatically. I am able to have the greatest confidence in his mercy, because of his consideration for my entire life. . . . It is neither a consequence of my evil will nor for a lack of opportunity that I have not fallen into far deeper misery, into far heavier debt, than that in which I currently find myself. God! we are such poor creatures that even a smaller measure of our wickedness must become a fount of our thankfulness to you.[12]

The inducement for this penitent disposition, and for the recording of his life up to that point, was the entanglements in which he became embroiled at this time, and upon which we must now focus, along with the principal moments of his early life.

Hamann was born on August 27, 1730, in Königsberg in Prussia; his father was a barber-surgeon [*Bader*] and, it seems, somewhat well-off.[13] The memory of his parents (R 1:152–55) "is among the dearest notions of his soul and is connected to the tender stirring of love and gratitude"; without further details about their character, it is said that the children (Hamann had only one younger brother) found "their home a school under supervision, indeed under strict supervision, via the example of their parents." His parents' house was a constant refuge for young students, which made the work decent; in this environment, Hamann occupied himself with languages (Greek, French, Italian), music, dancing, and painting. "As much as we scrimped on our rough-and-ready clothes and on other foolish things, so many excesses were given and provided to us in our education."[14] Hamann's education included seven years of instruction by a man who sought to teach him Latin without grammar instruction; thereafter he had a more methodical teacher, with whom he had to begin with Donatus's grammar.[15] The progress Hamann made then was such that this teacher flattered both himself and Hamann in the belief that he had trained a great scholar of Latin and Greek; Hamann calls him a pedant.[16] Beyond the skills obtained in the translation of Greek and Latin authors, in arithmetic, and in music, he [Hamann] indulges himself in the then-circulating opinion that education should be directed at the formation of understanding and judgment. Young nobles and many bourgeois children were to have as their texts for Latin and similar subjects textbooks about agriculture rather than the life of Alexander, etc.—opinions upon which the declamations and boastings of Basedow, Campe, and others, as well as their pompous enterprises, were based, and which have had such detrimental effects for the organization and the spirit of public education, that even now, however much we have turned away from these opinions, their consequences have not yet been fully remedied.[17] Hamann complains that he was left lacking in history and geography (for which, he laments, he could never properly compensate) and did not attain the slightest understanding of the poetic arts, such that it was a great effort for him to organize and readily express his thoughts in speech or in writing.[18] If a part of this lack is attributable to his instruction, the better part is attributable, as we will continue to see, to the otherwise characteristic temperament [*Temperatur*] and disposition of his spirit.

It is equally characteristic of him (although not of his instruction), as he further indicates, that all order, all perception and continuity, or even delight therein, are obfuscated in him. Overwhelmed with a multitude of words and matters with whose sense, foundation, context, and application he was not acquainted, he says, he lapsed into addiction, ever more without an alternative, without bringing together analysis and consideration. And this plague, he continues, spread to all of his activities;[19] in the remainder of his life he never matured in this respect, either. As a further error into which he lapsed he also names his childish impertinence and his curiosity to become knowledgeable about all kinds of heresies. "The enemy of our souls and of all that is good seeks to suffocate the divine wheat with his tares."[20] After further study, in which he received his first notions of philosophy and mathematics, of theology and Hebrew, there came a new field of excesses: "My brain became a fairground booth with brand-new wares"; in this maelstrom he entered the university in 1746. He was supposed to study theology, but found a hindrance in his tongue and poor memory, and many feigned hindrances in his mentality, etc. What removed him from his tastes for theology and for all the serious sciences was, he says, a new inclination which arose in him toward antiquities, criticism, then toward the so-called fine arts, poetry, novels, philology, the French writers and their gift for writing, for painting and portraying, for appealing to the imagination, etc. He prays ardently to God for forgiveness of this misuse of his natural strengths, etc. He avowed himself, therefore, "to the appearance of learnedness in the law, . . . without seriousness, without loyalty, to become a lawyer." His foolishness, he says, allowed him to see a kind of magnanimity and sublimity in studying not for one's bread, but according to inclination, as a pastime and out of love for the sciences themselves, since it was better to be a martyr than a day laborer and hireling of the muses. "What nonsense," he rightly adds against such arrogance, "can be expressed in round and euphonic words!"[21]

He now proposed to accept a post as a private tutor, in order to find the opportunity to try out his freedom, and also because he was kept somewhat short of money [in his parents' house]. He attributes the blame for his not dealing better with money to a lack of divine blessing, the "disorder, the general basic failing of my character, a false generosity, a love that was too blind, taking pleasure in the judgments of others, and a carelessness" born of inexperience.[22] He was soon cured only too well of his flaw of taking pleasure in the judgments of others.

As to the details of the disparities in which he became involved in his tutorial posts, we shall take up here only that which he blames upon his character. "My unsociable or strange manner of living," he says (R 1:177), "which was part pose, part false cleverness, part consequence of an inner

unrest with which I was ailing for a very long period of my life—a dis-
content and the inability to bear myself, the vanity to make myself into a
riddle—spoiled so much and made me offensive."[23] In his first post he
wrote two letters to the mother [of his pupil], a baroness in Livonia, which
were intended to awaken her conscience; her reply informed him of his
dismissal. It is reprinted to the letter on pages 254–55, the beginning of
which reads: "Herr Hamann: As you are in no condition whatsoever to be
educating children, and as the awful letters in which you paint my son in
such a mean and scurrilous light are in no way pleasing to me," etc. He
found some satisfaction for the humbling of his pride in the affection of
the child, in the self-flattery of his "innocence," and in the fact that his
good deeds were repaid with evil. "I wrapped myself," he said, "in the
cloak of religion and virtue, to cover my nakedness, but bristled with rage
to avenge and to justify myself"; but "this foolishness" soon evaporated.[24]
He fell into similar disparities in a second house,[25] and then into further
discord, in that he could not refrain, after having left the house, from
further forcing his epistolary instructions and repudiations upon both his
successor (a friend) and the pupils. His friend seemed to interpret this attention to the young baron as an infringement or a reproach, and repaid
Hamann with hatred and contempt.[26]

In Königsberg, Hamann had won the friendship of one of the *Berens*
brothers of Riga.[27] "He who knows and tests our hearts and can put them
to use had wise intentions when leading us, through each other, into
temptation."[28] Indeed, the complications with this friend and his family
are the most far-reaching element in Hamann's fate. He lived in their
house for a time, where he was regarded, he says, as a brother, almost as
an older brother; but he also admits that he could not abandon himself,
though he had every cause to be satisfied, to the joy of the company of
these most noble, lively, good-hearted people of both sexes; nothing but
mistrust toward himself and others, nothing but torment about how to
draw close to or disclose himself to them! He understands it as the work
of God's hand, now heavy above him, that he should *not know himself
amongst all the good* done unto him by these people whom he admired, respected, and befriended.[29] Hamann describes this condition of inner unrest as a depression which could not arrive, even in the presence of the
most well-meaning friendship (which he both received and recognized),
at an inner benevolence toward these friends, and thus not at any openness or frankness of relations with them. The French have a pithy expression for a person of this disagreeableness of disposition, aptly described
as maliciousness; they call such a person *un homme mal élevé*, in that they
correctly hold benevolence and openness to be the immediate conse-

quences of a good upbringing. Also indistinguishable in Hamann's youth is yet another seed of a later, higher self-education from the inside out (which is awaked in youth)—namely, there is no poetry in this stage of life, none of the imagination and passion, as it were, that contain a solid (though immature and ideal) interest in an object of intellectual activity, and are thus decisive for the whole of one's life. The energy of his intelligent nature becomes nothing more than a wild hunger for intellectual diversion which contains no purpose in which it might culminate. But the evil of his disposition would soon come to a head in a new test, and in a more severe manner.

He had returned to his second tutorial post in Courland for a short time. But called home to see his dying mother once more, and at the urging of intimate connections with the Berens house in Riga, he left that post again:[30] "God," he says (R 1:189), "gave the extraordinary blessing that I was released from the house in Courland with only the semblance of a reason and with no frankness, with the promise to return, which was a blatant lie and contrary to all my intentions and inclinations."[31] The connection with the Berens brothers was their admission of Hamann into their service, business, and family; he was to travel, at their expense, "to cheer myself up and to return to their house with more respect and more aptitude." After he had seen his mother die (about which he admits, despite the indescribable melancholy and sadness he felt, that his heart, at her deathbed, fell far short of the tenderness which he owed her, and further that he felt prepared, despite the imminent prospect of losing her, to abandon himself to other diversions in the world), he set out on October 1, 1756, equipped with money and authority, on a journey to *London,* via *Berlin* (where he made his first acquaintance with Moses Mendelssohn, among others), via Lübeck (where he spent the winter months with relatives), and Amsterdam.[32] In that city, he says, he lost all fortune to find acquaintances and friends of his own class or disposition, of which he had previously been so proud, such that he believed that everyone shunned him, and he shunned everyone; for this simple experience in a completely foreign Dutch city he sees no other reason than that God's hand was heavy above him, since he had removed God from his sight, confessing him only half-heartedly, etc. He was cheated out of money on the continued journey to London, by an Englishman whom he had found kneeling in prayer one morning and thus come to trust. In London, where Hamann arrived on April 18, 1757, his first course of action was to seek out a mountebank who he had heard could cure all defects of speech (such a defect had been mentioned earlier, probably a stutter). However, since the treatment seemed costly and protracted, Hamann did not engage in it and was forced, he says, to begin his business with his old tongue and his old heart.[33] He revealed this business (demanding payment of debts, it seems)[34] to those to whom he had been directed: "They were astonished at the importance of my affair, even more so at the manner of its execution, and perhaps most of all at the choice of the person to whom it had been entrusted"; he was simply smiled at and robbed of the hope of accomplishing anything. Hamann, however, duped himself into believing it now most wise "to do as little as possible in order not to pile up expenses, not to expose myself with overly hasty steps and make a fool of myself." So he wandered around, depressed and reeling, with no one to whom he could reveal himself, no one who could advise or help him, near desperation, and tried, for sheer amusement, to detain people and wear them down. "My intention was none other than to find an opportunity—and I would have taken anything for just that—to pay my debts and to be able to begin in a new folly; the empty attempts in which I awakened through letters, through the remonstrances of friendship and gratitude, were pure semblance, nothing but the imaginings of a knight-errant; and the bells of my fool's cap were my good humor and my valor."[35] Thus he describes the helplessness and weakness of his character. He finally sought out a coffeehouse, since he had no soul left to associate with, "that I might find some cheer in public society, in order perhaps in this way . . . to build a bridge to fortune." So completely downtrodden, due to the obstinacy of a loafing foolishness, spurning all composure and judiciousness, as well as the connection to his friends in Riga and to his father, we see him, after a year spent with absolutely no business or purpose, quartered, from February 8, 1758, on, in the house of a truly poor couple, where, in the course of three months, he ate properly four times at most, his entire subsistence consisting of gruel and a daily coffee. God, he says, allowed him to prosper extraordinarily, as he found himself, even with this nourishment, in good health; poverty, he adds, was the strongest motive for this diet, but also perhaps the only means of restoring his body from the consequences of gluttony.[36]

This inwardly and outwardly helpless situation drove him to seek out a *Bible;* here he describes the remorse which reading it brought forth in him, the recognition of the depth of divine will in the salvation of Christ, of his own crime and his life in the history of the Jewish people; his heart poured itself out in tears, he could no longer, could no longer conceal from his God that he was the fratricide, the murderer of God's begotten son.[37] We find in that time frequent accounts of the fear and torment which plagued people of simple, quiet lives when they could not fulfill the demand of penance and the condition of grace by finding, while searching inside, an abominable sinfulness in their hearts; but they eventually taught themselves that it was just this inability to discover sinfulness in themselves which was itself the most wicked sin, and [that they] had therefore progressed along the road to doing penance. After his account of his stay in London, Hamann had no need of such a conversion. Through his penance and repentance he now felt his heart more quieted than ever in his life; the consolation he received devoured all fear, all sadness, all mistrust, so that he could now find no trace of them in his heart. The next application he made of this new consolation was a fortification against the burden of his debts. He had squandered one hundred fifty pounds sterling in London; he owed just as much in Courland and Livonia. [He writes that] "his sins are debts of infinitely greater importance and consequence than his temporal ones; if the Christian is made right in God, in the main sense, then how should it matter to God that a trifle be offered up in addition." The three hundred pounds sterling are *his* debts; he leaves now to God all consequences of his sins, since God has taken the burden thereof upon himself.[38]

In this quieted mood he wrote this most characteristic account of his life and his heart, up to the end of April 1758, and also continued with it further from there.[39]

Letters from home and from Riga, which he received from a man who finally found him coincidentally on the street, led to the decision to return to Riga, where he arrived in July 1758 and was welcomed in the Berens house, he says, with every possible friendship and affection. He stays in that house; his affairs consist only of corresponding with a brother of the house, tutoring the oldest daughter of the head of the family, and offering minor assistance to a younger brother who worked in an office. He thanks God for blessing this work with a visible hand, and after a sleepless night spent in deliberation, he rose on December 15 with the intention to marry, having commended to the mercy of God himself and the young lady, a sister of his friend Herr Berens.[40] After receiving the permission of his father, he reveals his decision to the Berens brothers and to their sister herself, who seems in agreement. But the last day of the year 1758, Hamann writes (R 1:239), was full of extraordinary scenes between himself and one of the brothers, whom he hears speaking to him like *Saul among the prophets;* that was a day of suffering, of scolding and blaspheming. But he speaks edifyingly enough about the uncommon emotion of his change of mind(?) and the impressions of the mercy which he seemed to discern, and goes to bed glad to *die* that night if God will be so merciful as to save the *soul of this brother.*[41] In a letter to his father he describes the day of these scenes of Saulian prophet-speak, of suffering, of scolding, etc., as an end to a year of many extraordinary blessings which God has provided him.[42] With a penitent and unctuous prayer for all his friends, on the first day of the year 1759, his journal ends.[43] In that same letter to his father of January 9 he writes of his hope of receiving consent to the marriage from the one Berens brother who was in Petersburg and seems to have been the head of the family.[44] But the collection is incomplete here; the next letter of March 9 comes from Königsberg, and it makes evident that he has left Riga and that all connections with the Berens house have been severed for now. In the correspondence between Hamann and Rector J. G. *Lindner* in Riga, a common friend of Hamann and the Berens brothers,[45] those dark occurrences are no further elucidated. One does read enough, however, to see the full discord of both parties—as to the Berens brothers, their deep perception of the contrast between Hamann's foul conduct in England and the continuation of an idle life on the one hand, and the broad display of his piety and of the grace he had received from God on the other hand, particularly the pretension of his piety, his being so far ahead of his friends therein, and his desire that they recognize him as their master and apostle. Hamann had delivered his biography (which has now been characterized well enough here) into the hands of Herr Berens, it seems, following the marriage project and the contemporaneous explosions—for what purpose and further with what effects, it is clear enough; Berens expresses that he read this biography with disgust (R 1:362). In order not to die of hunger, Hamann had needed the Bible to overcome himself, and to return to Riga. On page 355, one even reads of Berens's threat to throw Hamann, *for his own good,* into a hole devoid of sun or moonlight.[46] The aforementioned *Lindner* and then also *Kant,* in the presence of one of the Berens brothers in Königsberg, whom business had brought there, made efforts, as common friends of both parties, to reconcile the dispute. Hamann's letters in this affair, particularly a few written to Kant, are among the most lively, open, and comprehensible things ever to have flown from his quill. Previously, Hamann's piety had had an attitude principally of penitence, inner joy, and devotion not only to God, but also an outward reassurance toward a relationship and good standing with his fellow man; now, in the crush of the dispute with his friends, the whole of his passion and his brilliant energy is aroused, and this passion and the independence of his temperament are added to this piety. Since Hamann's entire individuality, manner of representation, and style achieve their development within this half-year-long struggle and squabble, and since his literary career in earnest finds its origination here, we will linger in underscoring those attributes of this squabble which are most important for an understanding of his character; they are based upon a general, essential, and therefore entirely pervasive opposition.

Both parties insist upon and work toward a change of mind on the part of the other. Demanded of Hamann are respect, resolve, and an earnest entry into a life of judiciousness, usefulness, and industriousness; no attention is paid to the pretension of his piety, to the extent that this is not the cause of the foregoing. Hamann, on the other hand, fixes himself practically in the position of his inner confidence; his penitence and the faith he has attained via divine grace are the fortress in which he isolates himself, not only against the demands of his friends that he come to some common and solid understanding with them within the conditions of reality, and that he respect their objective principles, but also against their reproaches, turning the tables, giving up the hope that they will come to some self-knowledge, and demanding of them penance and conversion instead. The common point which holds them together is the bond of friendship, which remained, at least for Hamann, it seems, unshakeable even despite all their differences; but his claiming rights and duties from them also represents a rejection of everything which they assert against him, such that he does not allow them to approach him. The principle from which he derives his dialectic is the religious one, which abstractly asserts his superiority over so-called earthly duties and over activity in and for existing relationships, and which confines his haphazard personality within this superiority—a dialectic which becomes in this matter sophistry. The following emphasizes the chief characteristics thereof, with some demonstration of the peculiar way in which Hamann's humor is thus expressed.

At first, his friends *Lindner* and *Kant* come off quite poorly in their mediations. When the former, wishing to be an impartial middleman, relays the remarks of his friend Berens, Hamann asks whether it can be called neutrality when one takes in armed men under the cover of his letters and renders his envelope a Trojan horse. He parallels this favor [Lindner has done for Berens] with that of a Herodias for her mother, asking for the head of John the Baptist; he calls it approaching him as a hypocrite in sheep's clothing, etc.[47] Of Kant's efforts, Hamann writes to him (July 27, 1759): "I almost laugh at the choice of a philosopher for the purpose of bringing forth a change of mind in me. I regard the best demonstration as a reasonable girl regards a love letter, and an explanation à la Baumgarten as a witty *fleurette*."[48] Most characteristically, Hamann expressed his position in this struggle such that Kant, having been pulled into the affair, was in danger of "coming so close to a person given, by *the sickness of his passion, a strength* in thinking and in feeling *which a healthy person does not possess.*"[49] This is a trait which is apt for the entire peculiarity of Hamann. The letters to Kant are written with a particular and great passion. It seems that he had not answered Hamann's first or later letters, and Hamann had heard that Kant found his pride to be unbearable. About this pride and about Kant's silence he writes further to Kant, provoking him with long-winded vehemence; he asks whether Kant will raise himself up to his [Hamann's] pride, or whether he should condescend to Kant's vanity.[50]

To the reproaches made against him on account of his previous behavior and his current lack of direction, he replies simply, with the parrhesia of confession and admission, that he is the noblest of sinners; in just this perception of his weakness lies the comfort which he enjoyed in his salvation. To the humiliation piling up against him in the form of these reproaches, he rejoins with pride in the old rascals who have rescued him from out of the pit, and he goes on to say that he flaunts this as gladly as Joseph in his coat of many colors.[51] To the specific concern his friends show for his situation and future, his impracticality and unemployment, he responds that he is destined to be neither statesman nor merchant nor sophisticate; instead he thanks God for the peace which he has given him. After leaving Riga, Hamann lived with his aged father, who, he says, gives him everything abundantly for his nourishment and necessity. He who is free and can be free, he says, should not become a servant, so he walked alongside his aged father and did not ask what advantage or derogation his own presence presented for him. *Reading the Bible and praying is the work of a Christian,* he says, and his soul, with all of its moral deficiencies and base crookedness, is in God's hands.[52] Should one still want to know what he was up to, he claims to be *Lutherizing;* after all, something had to be done. "This venturesome monk said in Augsburg(!): here I stand—I cannot do otherwise. God help me, Amen!"[53] He initially settles his debts with the Berenses thus (in the one letter to Kant, R 1:444): should the matter come up, Kant should tell Berens that Hamann has nothing and is living only by the mercy of his father; should he die, he says, he wants to bequeath his corpse to Herr Berens, which Berens, then, like the Egyptians, could distrain. He writes to the Berenses a year later (R 3:17–18) to put their claim to his debts in order, and receives settlement in the reply that his previous departure from their home shall be the quittance of all liabilities ever existing between them.[54]

The primary turn in his behavior toward his friends, however, is his reversing the charge to be against them, his demand that one of the brothers, in light of all the deep discoveries he had made about Hamann's heart, should feel it in *his own bosom* and recognize himself as a *mishmash of great spirit* and *miserable ninny,* as he had supposedly declared to Hamann with much flattery (Berens's flattery, Hamann says, hurt him more than his previous biting incursions) and candor.[55] In this private matter, he says, he only overburdened his *friend Lindner* so, against his conscience and duty, because he wished and hoped that Lindner would thus realize the *application of it all for his own life.* How often, Hamann says, was he reminded of the suffering of our Redeemer, when his neighbors and friends [*Tischfreunde*] *heard nothing* and did not know *what he was saying* and what he wanted to *give them to understand.*[56] He was charged severely with disprizing his means; but he would otherwise have been a dispraiser of the holy order. And what better means could his friend have asked of God than *him,* an old, true friend come in his *own* name? Since *they did not know, however, him who had sent him,* Hamann too was rejected, as soon as *he came in his name;* they reject him whom *God has sealed in the service of their souls.* His friends might sicken at the incoherent fare which they find in his letters, but what did he read in theirs? Nothing but the fruits of his own flesh and blood, which is more depraved than theirs— nothing but the snarling of his own old Adam which he is castigating with his own satires, the wounds of which he himself felt more so than they, retained longer than they, grumbled and cooed about more than they, because, by their own admission, he claims, *he possesses more life, more affect, more passion* than they.[57]

The calling which God has assigned to him, namely helping his friends along toward self-knowledge, he further confirms by claiming that just as the tree is known by its fruits, so he knows himself to be a prophet— by his *fate,* which he *shares with all witnesses,* to be slandered, persecuted, and despised;[58] the highest level of *worship* which *hypocrites bring to God* (he tells his friends another time) consists in the *persecution of true confessors.*[59] In accordance with this arrogated status, he challenges Kant (R 1:505) to rebuff him with the same force, and to defy his own prejudices, just as Hamann has attacked Kant and his prejudices; otherwise, Kant's love of truth and virtue will be, in Hamann's eyes, as contemptible as a paramour's arts.[60] At times he indicates that the entire quarrel is nothing more than a collective examination of their hearts, his included. In a letter to *Lindner* (R 1:375–76), for example, he writes: Lindner should *judge* what Hamann says, and should consider the tribunal of his neighbor as a chastisement from the Lord, that we may not be damned together with the rest of the world.[61] As a Christian, Lindner should, Hamann writes, forgive the wounds which Hamann had to inflict upon him, the pain he had to cause. As he writes on page 353, Hamann does not recognize the vehemence in the letters of his friend Berens; he sees everything as the effect of his friendship, and sees this in turn as a gift and as a test from God. Hamann asserts that he wrote (R 1:393) in an uncommonly bitter tone only "so that your inclination, your heart for us might be made known before God; God wanted to test what kind of emotions the love of Christ would bring forth in my heart toward you, and what the love of Christ in you would bring forth toward us."[62]

Concerning his challenge to Kant and the pretension of subjecting himself, with his friends, to the community of scrutiny, his confidence in his own perfection through penance and his superiority over his friends is, as we have shown, so strongly expressed that these friends could not have experienced anything other than Hamann's own "pride." Of course, these premises of his made it impossible for any understanding to be reached. As previously mentioned, it seems that Kant had already refused to become further involved with Hamann in this matter; Hamann's last letter to Kant (R 1:504–14) reproaches him for his silence and tries to force explanations from him. Hamann likewise feels that his efforts to impress his other friends Lindner and Berens are in vain (R 1:469: "All my siren's arts are in vain," etc.), and further suggests (R 1:495–96), since the correspondence between them might rather degenerate more and more, that they abandon this matter and let it rest for awhile instead.[63] In fact, Hamann's experience here is not lost on him; from now on we see in him a modified, sensible demeanor toward Lindner (with whom his correspondence was taken up again after some time)[64] and toward later friends—a demeanor which is predicated on the equality of the right of moral and religious features, and which leaves the freedom of his friends unimpaired and unharried.

But this relinquishment of his attendance to his friends' hearts, of pressing them to discuss the condition of their souls, is more of an outward appearance, and extends only to his direct behavior toward them. His drive to be recognized as a teacher and a prophet is now directed (since he must give it up in his correspondences) toward another means by which he can have his say: by means of his publications. Already in the final letters to Lindner and especially to Kant, we see the seeds and then the specific declaration of the *Socratic Memorabilia,* the beginning of his authorship, as Hamann himself calls this work.[65] He positions the younger Berens, together with Kant, over against himself, in the relationship of Alcibiades to Socrates, and seeks permission to speak as the *Genius.*[66] In a completely characteristic, highly spirited letter to Kant, he adopts the turn (R 1:437–38) that he (Hamann) has as little to do with truth as do Kant's friends; "Like Socrates, I believe everything which the other believes and only intend to *disturb others in their belief.*"[67] In the other frequently cited letter to Kant (R 1:506), his reproach is that Kant has made no effort to understand or misunderstand him. Since his [Hamann's] own offering had been to play the role of the child, Kant should have questioned him; Hamann says he had striven by all means to evoke such an engagement, with the purpose of bringing his friend to self-knowledge.[68] The *Socratic Memorabilia* are the execution and explicit exposition of the position he wishes to take: that of Socrates, who had been unknowing and had exposed his ignorance in order to draw his fellow citizens in and to lead them to self-knowledge and to a wisdom which lies hidden. In retrospect, one sees that Hamann was no happier with the idiosyncratic purpose of this text than with his letters; it apparently had no further effect on Kant and did not lead to any engagement on his part. In fact, it seems that the *Memorabilia* incurred for Hamann only the contempt and scorn of his adversaries. But not only does this work express the general impetus behind Hamann's collected works, from it are also created the principles which later brought forth a general effect. Thus, we will linger here awhile, but not before noticing that Hamann did not even take the trouble, for purposes of this text, to read up on Plato and Xenophon, as he himself admits somewhere.[69]

In the dedication—which is doubled: to *Nobody*, the Notorious (the Public), and to *Two*[70]—he characterizes them, Berens and Kant (R 2:7): "The first works like a friend of man [*Menschenfreund*] on the philosopher's stone, believing it a means to promote *industriousness, bourgeois virtues*, and the *common good* . . . The other would like to seem as *universal a philosopher* and as *competent a Warden of the Mint* as Newton was."[71] Socrates himself (i.e., Hamann) remained unknowing, regardless of the succession of taskmasters sent to him; but "he exceeded the others in wisdom, since he was farther along in self-knowledge than they, and he *knew* that he *knew nothing*. With this *I know nothing!* he turned away the learned and curious Athenians and facilitated for his lovely lads the disavowal of their vanity, seeking to gain their trust through his equality with them. All of Socrates' *ideas,* which were *nothing but emissions* and *secretions of his ignorance,* seemed to the Sophists, to the scholars of his time, as appalling as the hair on the head of Medusa, the navel of the aegis."[72] From this ignorance he proceeds to say that our *own existence* and the *existence of all things* outside us must be *believed* and constituted in no other manner. "Faith," he says, "is not the work of reason and cannot therefore be subject to any onslaught thereof, as *believing* [*Glauben*] comes about just as little from reason as do *tasting* and *seeing.*"[73] There is no more honorable seal for the Socratic attestation of his ignorance, he says, than 1 Corinthians 7: "Anyone who claims to know something does not yet have the necessary knowledge; but anyone who loves God is known by him." And, from ignorance, "from this death, from this nothingness, the life and essence of a higher knowledge shoots forth, newly created—this far, the nose of a Sophist does not reach."[74]

"The peculiarities of his manner of teaching and thinking are the natural consequences of this Socratic ignorance. What could be more natural than this, that he felt himself compelled always to ask in order to become wiser; that he pretended to be credulous, accepted every opinion as true, and preferred to employ the *test of mockery* and *good humor* rather than an earnest examination, . . . spoke *ideas,* as he did not understand *dialectic;* . . . that he, like all fools, often spoke so *confidently* and *decisively,* as if he were the only one among all the night-owls of his fatherland who sat on Minerva's helmet."[75] We see how Hamann groups Socrates and himself together stylistically as well; the final strokes of this figure suit Hamann himself more so than Socrates. This is also true, unmistakably, of the following: "Socrates answered the accusation made against him with such gravity and courage, with such pride and cool-headedness, that one could have taken him for the commander of his judges rather than the accused." "Plato interprets Socrates' *voluntary poverty* as a sign of his divine sending. A greater sign is his share in the final fate of *prophets* and *the righteous*" (Matthew 23:29; see above: to be slandered and ridiculed).[76]

The tenor of Hamann's other writings is not as wholly personal as the tenor, content, and purpose of this text (although it is given, for the public, the appearance of an objective content), but in all of them we find the interest and the tenor of his personality more or less mixed in. The statements about *faith,* as well, are in a similar way taken primarily from the Christian faith, but extended to a universal sense, such that the *sensory certainty* of outward, temporal things—"of our own being and of the existence of all things"—is also called a *faith.*[77] In this extension, *Jacobi's* principle of faith, as is generally known, became the principle of a philosophy, and one recognizes in Jacobi's statements almost verbatim those of Hamann. The broad claim which religious faith has only in the right and power of its absolute content is thus expanded to subjective believing with the particularity and haphazardness of its relative and finite content. The relationship of this contortion, too, to Hamann's character in general will further unfold in what follows.

Second Article

Before we continue to trace *Hamann's* literary career, we should briefly attend to some remaining circumstances of his biography.[78] The prolific collection of letters which is disclosed to the public here (especially those directed to J. G. *Lindner* and, when these terminate, to *Herder,* as well as those to a few other men with whom Hamann came into contact) portray many sides of this generally quite simple life with the complete singularity in which Hamann finds himself; we must, nonetheless, limit ourselves to the dry succession of the facts.

As we have said, after leaving the Berenses' house in January of 1759, Hamann lived with neither employment nor purpose in the home and at the expense of his father. Hamann's only brother, who had been employed in Riga as a schoolteacher, was likewise brought back into his father's house, as he had fallen into a melancholy which rendered him unfit for his office and which eventually developed into complete mental deficiency; Hamann had, at eighteen years of age, already been burdened with the care and guardianship of his brother.[79] Among the events from this time, a relationship into which Hamann entered is made memorable by his peculiarity, which otherwise would really have carried no particular interest. In 1763 he entered into a marriage of conscience (as he himself sometimes called it) with a farm girl who seems not to have distinguished herself in any way. The relationship resulted in many children, and he remained in it his entire life.[80] Our editor says (preface to vol. 3) that respect prohibits him from including in the present collection Hamann's memorable communications about the origin of this relationship, but that provision would be made that they should not vanish. Yet there is certainly enough to be found in the present collection to satisfy any curiosity. We are not given to know the sentiments that led Hamann to this second decision in quite the manner in which we experienced his frame of mind during his previously described decision to ask for the hand of the Berenses' sister. Where his journal speaks (R 1:237) of those stirrings that led to his earlier intentions, he thanks God "that I am freed from the appeals of the flesh," and asks that it may continue to be so in the future. In a diction which befits the incoherence of this half-dreaming state, he says that he was so aware of his inability to sleep, that he heard a voice within himself asking him about this decision to take a wife. "Out of obedience to him—I spoke not a word. But it seemed as if I leapt up with a yell and screamed: '*If I should,* then give me no other.'"[81] He adds: "Yes, since God watched over me . . . with a special attention, I could not have sinned in any commingling of the flesh, even if my body should be as good as dead.

Abraham believed and did not waver. Does he not give children to the lonely; can he not raise them up out of stone?"[82] About modifications of his sentiment during the second relationship (which, as we have said, was accompanied by a rich blessing of children), and about the origination of it, he makes quite candid statements to Herder and later to Franz von Buchholtz (about whom we will have more to say later). In a letter to the latter (of September 7, 1784; R 7:162) he recounts quite simply the fondness he has developed for this country girl who had come into his father's house as a maid. "Her blossoming youth, health as strong as an oak, virile innocence, simplicity, and loyalty brought forth in me such a hypochondriac rage that neither religion, reason, fortune, nor medicine, fasting, renewed journeys, nor diversions could overcome it."[83] Regarding the irregularity of living with her forever in extramarital circumstances, he declares to Herder about this part of his life's story, now entering its seventeenth year, as follows (R 5:193–94): "Despite the great contentment in which I live and which constitutes my entire happiness, I feel strongly the element of the bourgeois mischief" (of his marriage of conscience, or whatever one wants to call *living as one will*). "Even the farm girl whose full-blooded, blossoming health and equally squarely headstrong, stupid honesty and constancy made such an impression on me that absence and the tests of the highest distress and coldest reflection have not been able to extinguish it—this girl, who has been like his own child to my poor, destitute, lame father, and whom he has loved as his own daughter . . . , might become as my wife I know not what. Not out of pride (for that I am thankful), but because I have the inner conviction that this situation could diminish her own happiness and perhaps the happiness of her own children."[84]

Perhaps this relationship of Hamann's in the house of his father also contributed to the latter's decision early in 1763 to share the division of his mother's wealth with both his sons (R 3:183). Hamann was busy at this time with the composition of several minor essays—following the *Socratic Memorabilia*—and with critiques for the *Königsberger Zeitung* [*Königsberg Newspaper*] (which our editor has meticulously sought out and added to the collection; they are really nothing of significance), as well as with the most colorful reading. Hamann is now induced to care for himself and to look around for work other than praying and reading the Bible, which he had previously indicated to be the work of a Christian. God gave him, as he puts it (R 3:184), the occasion to think of his own cot: "He who was also there when I lay down in Hell, and who helped me to overcome the *shame of leisure,* he will also be with me now even in the danger of my affairs."[85] In volume 3, his supplication of July 29, 1763, to the Royal Prussian Chamber of War and Domain in Königsberg is printed on page 207, in which he indicates that a slow tongue and an inability to articulate, along with an equally delicate disposition and constitution, render him unfit for most public service, and that he can rely on neither any earnings nor any qualifications other than his ability *in an emergency to write legibly and to calculate a little.* He asks to be allowed a probation of his voluntary services, so that he might in this way be favored, as an *Invalid of Apollo,* with a post as a customs official [*Zöllner*].[86] But half a year later he asks, in "complete despair of the possibility of ever mastering a copyist's hand or the visual judgment necessary for it," to be relieved of his duties (R 3:210–11), and takes on the editorship of a scholarly journal.[87] Hamann had come into contact with Herr *von Moser* via a statement which he had made (in the *Crusades of a Philologian,* R 2:149) about the latter's pamphlet "The Lord and the Servant," which was causing quite a stir at the time.[88] Hamann now hoped, by utilizing Moser, to obtain employment (R 3:205; "with a truly respectable salary as a teacher of boredom [*der langen Weile*]"),[89] and thus traveled in June, seemingly without inquiring with Herr von Moser ahead of time, and without informing him of this intention, to Frankfurt am Main, from which Moser had departed for a long trip four days before Hamann's arrival. Hamann, who could not tarry until Moser's return, came back to Königsberg at the end of September with neither skill nor direction.[90] In June of 1767 he was engaged as a clerk and translator [*Secrétaire-Interprète*] by the Provincial Excise and Customs Office of Königsberg, with an initial monthly salary of sixteen thalers, which was later raised to thirty thalers, but then fell back to twenty-five thalers.[91] While holding this office, he lost, primarily through the purchase of many books, the greater part of the assets which had fallen to him upon his father's death. He brought his economic status (a debt of 600 fl.) before Herr von Moser (R 5:57–58),[92] probably at the latter's urging; pages 166f. would seem to indicate that Hamann found help from him.[93] Later, Herder helps him magnanimously out of a pecuniary embarrassment, which would otherwise have compelled him to sell his library.[94] At the end of 1774, he again has to work as a "dispatching copyist" (R 5:95); cf. R 4:242–43, where he also mentions the circumstance, in a *Letter to the Public,* that he received his monthly salary of seven hundred fifty düttchen paid out in token coins which were not accepted by the post office (postage represented for him a considerable expense).[95] At the beginning of 1777, he was finally appointed administrator of the customs warehouse (R 5:216–17); his salary was the same, three hundred reichsthalers, but he also had a free apartment and garden and a share of the so-called *Foigelder* which amounted to more than one hundred reichs-thalers, with which he now meant to be "content and happy, if Satan's envy does not spoil the exquisite salve of contentment."[96] His ample vexations about the garden can be seen in the letters to his friend the conductor Reichardt in Berlin, whose assistance he called upon in official matters, albeit in vain.[97] He was further troubled by the loss of that subsidy from the *Foigelder,* so that he found himself always in hard-pressed circumstances (although his position had been relieved somewhat at the end of 1778 upon the death of his unfortunate brother and the passing of his brother's assets to him) on account of his large family, his addiction to purchasing books, and considerable losses from the sale of multiple homes into which he had plunged his assets,[98] circumstances (R 5:287; "The mind full of base, groveling, earthly concerns for food")[99] which he nevertheless bore perseveringly with the tranquility and serenity of his character on account of his thrift, his Christian valor, and his singular humor, not to mention much assistance from friends. Moreover, he attests often that the post as customs warehouse administrator was the only office in the land which he would have desired. According to the bon mot of a former royal Prussian license-customs warehouse master, all other public servants had only donkey's labor and siskin's feed; he, however, was the only exception, having donkey's feed and siskin's labor (R 5:210).[100] He had little work to do, or in his own words, none at all, "basically neither any business nor any responsibility" (R 6:193); "rather, I am spoiled by too much comfort, too much peace and leisure." The time which he had to spend at his station (R 6:218–19), from 7:00 in the morning until 12:00 noon and again from 2:00 until 6:00 in the evening, he devoted primarily to reading.[101] These readings are remarkably variegated, without any sense of purpose, all random and disordered; hence they had more of a negative impact than a formative influence on his writings. An approximate list of the books which he mentions in his letters of summer 1781 will provide an example. On April 8 he finished the fifty-four volumes of Voltaire; then the first thirty fascicles of Kant's *Critique of Pure Reason; Le procès des trois rois,* London 1780; then eighteen more fascicles of Kant; *Des erreurs et de la vérité;* Locke, *On Human Understanding; Histoire privée de Louis XV;* Herder's *Theological Letters,* etc.; then Buffon's *Histoire des oiseaux;* the *Bibliotheca Fratrum Polonorum;* Zeltner's *Historia arcani Cryptosoinianismi Altdorfini,* etc.[102] This reading addiction could only be even less fruitful after he wrote to Lavater (in 1778, R 5:280): "It has long been the case that I only enjoy an author for as long as I have his book in my hand. As soon as I close it, everything flows together in my soul, as if my memory were blotting paper."[103]

His other activities included teaching Greek, English, Italian, etc., to his children and also to other acquaintances,[104] as well as associating with friends in Königsberg—J. G. Lindner, who had been sent there, and Hippel and Kant, with whom he was on good terms, if soon somewhat remote and not entirely intimate (not only had Hippel not entrusted the authorship of his *Lives* [*in an Ascending Line*][105] to Hamann, he had expressly denied it to him), and with a few others, such as Kreutzfeld, Kraus, etc.[106]— as well as corresponding with friends elsewhere, and finally writing and other commonplaces of life.

The experience which we previously narrated in detail had finally dissuaded Hamann from appointing himself preacher of punishment and penance to his friends, and taught him also to get along with those people to whom his inner self must remain alien. Similarly, poverty had led him to accept a post and employment which was completely heterogeneous to his spirit and his skills, but which was also perhaps more fitting than that relationship in which he could have remained with his friends in Riga, inasmuch as a completely superficial and dull trade left the stubbornness of his abstract character unchallenged, whereas a situation of wittier activity and a more concrete position among people would have encouraged him to abandon his isolation and situate himself in more sensible community. So we see him now in a comfortable and peaceful relationship with old school friends, as well as with those who acquired his books for him, despite the great difference between his and their peculiarity. He is able to grant his company to such men as *Kraus* and the war councilor *Scheffner,* who desired to present his vast shallowness to the public in the biography left behind after his death.[107] It is the same phenomenon as that previously mentioned: that the strangest reading, whose content could have held no interest for him, occupied and amused him in the face of the idleness and boredom of his official vegetation.

Friendship was an important matter in the affairs of the scholars and literati of that time, as we see in the many correspondences which have since been printed. The comparison of the different types and fortunes of these friendships could most likely provide an interesting array of characteristics, particularly if one wanted to draw a parallel between these correspondences and the equally numerous volumes of printed letters of the French literati of the time.

Hamann's religious turn had taken the form of an abstract interiority whose stubborn simplicity neither recognizes objective regulations, duties, or theoretical or practical principles as essential per se, nor takes the slightest interest in these things. A disagreement in this regard, though it can of course go quite a way, cannot disturb a friendship born of a common foundation primarily through happenstance and subjective inclination; thus, another of Hamann's key characteristics is his constancy in friendship. It is interesting to hear him explain his notion of friendship, which he does multiple times, especially during the major dispute with his friends which we described earlier. To his mind, the most severe reproaches, the most passionate pronouncements are mere tests (R 1:391); friendship is for him a gift from God, inasmuch as everything which seems to aim at its destruction brings about nothing but its refinement and preservation.[108] Friendship, for him, has nothing to do with teaching, instructing, repenting, or proselytizing. What then, he asks, is the quality of friendship? "To love, to feel, to suffer. But what will love, feeling, passion supply or teach a friend? Faces, miens, raptures, figures, actions that speak, stratagems, enthusiasm, jealousy, rage." Further: "I would be a most abject and ungrateful person if I let myself be frightened away quickly by the coldness of my friend, by his misunderstanding, or even by *his apparent enmity,* from remaining his friend. Under all these circumstances, it is even more so my duty to bear it up, and to wait until it pleases him to bestow upon me again his previous trust."[109] So Hamann maintains throughout his life the same warm disposition toward the Berens brothers with whom he had had such bitter associations. There are awakened in Hamann also, following *Mendelssohn's* death, earlier affections toward him. To Mendelssohn, at least the beginning of Hamann's literary career had not appeared contemptible. Hamann convinces himself, after all the ferocity with which he had exploded against Mendelssohn, that he has remained his friend, and that he still could have convinced him of that fact.[110]

With *Herder,* at least, he maintains a continuous (though often quite stilted or even satirical) tone of intimate friendship. Despite this friendship, Hamann tells Herder at one point (R 5:61) that which is otherwise evident enough, namely that their respective points of view and horizons are too disparate and dissimilar to compromise on certain issues. He "*damns*" one of the prize essays (R 5:77) which had won Herder much fame. About his work on the apocalypse, Hamann writes to Herder (R 6:103) on October 29, 1779, that this book is the first one which he can love and praise with the fullness of his heart and mouth[111]—which means even less given the more remote relationship between that book and the fullness of heart and spirit. It is a generic trait, and not a sign of goodwill, that Hamann becomes so agitated precisely by the writings of his best friends that he attacks them in essays intended for publication, charged with his usual manner of passionate virulence and mischief, which are themselves not without a component which can be perceived as bitter scorn, and can be quite insulting. Hamann had written a brief notice in the *Königsberger Zeitung* about Herder's prize essay on the origin of languages, disavowing, not always obliquely, the main idea of Herder's book.[112] But he also wrote an extremely severe essay entitled *Philological Ideas and Doubts*, etc. (R 4:37–72),[113] in which he expresses his doubts, no less strongly than before, as to whether the author ever seriously intended to prove his subject or even *to touch* upon it. The criteria for this doubt are found, Hamann claims, in the fact that the entire argument (about the human origins of language) consists of a round circle, eternal spinning, and *absurdity which is neither veiled nor subtle,* and is based upon the cryptic powers of arbitrary names and societal passwords, pet ideas, etc.[114] However, Hamann abstained from publishing this essay after Herder, having heard about it, expressed the wish that it not be brought before the public. Hamann also left unpublished a notice of Kant's *Critique of Pure Reason,* written for the *Königsberger Zeitung,*[115] along with his essay *Metacritique,* to which we will return later. We will also touch later upon the fact that Jacobi's writings about his disagreements with Mendelssohn, the *Letters on Spinoza,* etc. (from which Jacobi reaped much benefit), met with no mercy from Hamann.

Related to this particular sort of friendship is the peculiarity of Hamann's piety, the basic feature of his writings and of his life, as we will now specify more fully. We saw him earlier in the religious sentiment of his external and internal misery, which soon passed over into the joyfulness of a reconciled heart, so that the torture and accursedness of a mind which perennially carries in itself the conflict between religious demands and the contradictory consciousness of sinfulness was overcome. But that sanctimonious language and the contrarious tone which tended more toward the language of hypocrisy than toward piety are already found in their fullest measure in that which has been drawn out of his biography from this period, and in the essay[116] itself. It appears more and more that Hamann lapsed into hypocrisy, as he, having absolved himself inwardly of his sins, now not only pesters his friends with the confession that he is the greatest of sinners, but further answers to them for his starving, directionless, and lazy lifestyle with the pantheism of false religiosity, namely that it is all God's will. "The Christian," he writes to his friends, "does everything in God. Eating and drinking, traveling from one city to another, staying there for a year and doing business and walking about or sitting still and waiting" (referring to his stay in England), "these are all *divine* affairs."[117] He would not have failed to find a pleasurable circle of friends with whom to refresh and glorify himself in the haze of smug sinfulness. *Goethe* tells in his *Life* how "the Quiet Ones in the Land"[118] around Frankfurt at that time turned their attention to Hamann and became acquainted with him, how these pious people thought Hamann to be pious in the same way and treated him with reverence as "the Magus from the North," but then soon took offense at his *Clouds*[119] and even more at the title page of his *Crusades of a Philologian,* upon which is shown in extreme ridiculousness the goatish profile of a horned Pan, as well as at another satirical woodcut (both of which are to be found in this edition, R 2:103, 134) of a large rooster, beating time for the young chickens which stand before him with sheet music in their claws[120]—whereupon these people indicated to Hamann their uneasiness. But he simply withdrew from them. Hamann probably could have found new friends of the same kind in his area, and if the temperament of his brother, which ended in idiocy, furnished him with a further probability that he would follow the path of hypocrisy, he was saved from it by the strong and fresh root of friendship in his mind, by the ingenious vitality of his spirit and his nobler temperament. This root of friendship did not allow him to be dishonest with himself or with his friends, nor to spurn the principle of worldly judiciousness. A strongly positive element, a firm wedge driven through his heart, was required to overcome its stubbornness; but his stubbornness was not killed, its energetic vitality rather absorbed completely into piety. Hamann has a certain awareness of this, so that he even thanks God (R 1:373) that he is "wonderfully made."[121]

In the frequently cited argument with his friends, he expresses this connection between his piety and his peculiar vitality many times. He says (R 1:393): "As Paul wrote to the Corinthians in such a grim and singular tone" (which he parallels with his own conduct), "what a *mixture of passions* must this have achieved in the minds of both Paul and the Corinthians? Responsibility, anger, fear, desire, zeal, vengeance. If natural man has five senses, then the Christian is an instrument with ten strings and, *without passions,* resembles a clanging more than a new man."[122] This piety, which also carries within itself the worldly element of an eminent genius, differed essentially from the manners of a small-minded pietistic, mawkish, or fanatical piety, but also from the quieter, more unprejudiced piety of a righteous Christian, and further allowed others who did not belong to the "Quiet Ones in the Land" to be in acceptant community with him.

Of interest with respect to Hamann, our editor makes note (R 3:vi–vii) of a book which Hamann's longtime friend G. I. Lindner published in 1817,[123] in which Lindner provides a description of Hamann and says with regard to his religiosity that his admirable and adroit mental powers, not mere idiosyncrasies, were the cause of the *enthusiasm* in his moral and religious way of thinking. He was, Lindner adds, "*the strong de-*

fender of the crassest orthodoxy."[124] This is the name used at that time to refer to the essential doctrine of Christianity in the Protestant church. The name "orthodoxy" later vanished, together with the name "hetero-doxy" (the latter having been given to the ideas of the Enlightenment), since these ideas have almost ceased to be anything divergent, and are instead virtually the common doctrine not only of so-called rationalistic theology, but also of so-called exegetical theology and especially of sentimental theology. Hamann was likely aware of the *objective* correlation of the reconciliation which his mind attained, which correlation is the Christian doctrine of the *triune nature of God.* It stands in the starkest contrast to Hamann's faith, and to the Lutheran and Christian faith at large, when modern-day practitioners of theology still want to be devoted to the Christian doctrine of reconciliation, while denying that the doctrine of triunity is the very foundation of reconciliation; without this objective foundation, the doctrine of reconciliation can only have a subjective meaning. This foundation stands firm for Hamann. In a letter to *Herder* (R 5:242) he writes: "Without the so-called mystery of the Holy Trinity, not one teaching of Christianity seems possible to me; beginning and end fall away." He speaks in this context of a book which he had with him at that time, and says that that which is called the *pudenda* of religion (precisely that which others call cross orthodoxy), along with the superstition to circumcise it, and the madness to excise it altogether, will be the content of this embryo.[125] But another idea tends to be aligned with orthodoxy, namely that it is a faith which a person carries inside himself only as a dead formula, external to the spirit and the heart. No one was further removed from this idea than Hamann; his faith rather carried in itself the contrast that it proceeded to utterly concentrated, formless vitality. This is expressed most clearly in *Jacobi's* (*Exquisite Correspondence,* 2:142) statement about Hamann, in a "Letter to F. L. Count von Stolberg."[126] Hamann once whispered in my ear, he writes: "All clinging to words and literal teachings of religion is *Lama-Worship.*" Hamann was not otherwise in the habit of whispering his parrhesia; the intellectual manner of his piety gives consistent evidence of freedom from the death of formulas. Among many others, the following more direct passage from a letter from Hamann to *Lavater* from 1778 (R 5:276–78) is of note. In opposition to Lavater's *inner disquietude, incertitude, and thirst,* and to his *external busyness,* whose impetus was found in his struggle with the above and indeed with himself, Hamann synthesizes the commandment of his own Christian disposition thusly: "Eat your bread with joy, drink your wine with a merry heart, for your work pleases God. Live joyfully with the wife whom you love, all the days of your vain life that he has given you under the sun[127] . . . Your (Lavater's) *knots of doubt* are phenomena just as ephemeral as our system of heaven and earth, including every vexatious copying and adding machine."[128] He adds: "To speak to you from the depths of my soul, my entire Christianity is a taste for *signs* and for the elements of water, bread, and wine. Here is a fullness of hunger and thirst, a fullness which is not merely a shadow of the goods to come, like the *law*, but rather αὐτὴν τὴν εἰκόνα τῶν πραγμάτων,[129] inasmuch as it is shown through a mirror in a riddle[130] but can be made *present* and *concrete;* the τέλειον[131] lies beyond."[132] That which Hamann calls his taste for signs is this: that everything *objectively* present only applies, for him, to his own internal and external situations, as to history and doctrines, insofar as it is composed of spirit, created for spirit, such that this divine meaning is neither the thought nor the image of an enthusiastic fantasy, but rather the only truth [*das Wahre*], which thus has present actuality. It is in this context that our editor, in the aforementioned passage, stresses this book by G. I. *Lindner.*[133] Lindner further explains there that he once expressed to Hamann his feelings about Hamann's interpretations of rather neutral Bible passages, namely that given Hamann's original talents and protean wit, he (Lindner) could have turned dirt into gold and straw huts into fairy palaces. He further wanted to sublimate from the filth of Crébillonian novels, etc., everything which Hamann glossed and interpreted from every line of the Chronicles, from Ruth, from Esther, etc. Hamann, he says, replied: *We are counting on it.*[134]

Since Hamann's faith contained a positive foundation as its postulate, this foundation was for him something solid but something divine, neither an externally present thing ([like] the Host of the Catholics), nor a doctrinal formula contained in literal words (as in the literal faith of orthodoxy), nor even an external historicity of memory. Rather, this positive is only the beginning of his faith, essential to its animating application, for its formation, expression, and concretization. Hamann knows that this animating principle is essentially [one's] own individual spirit, and that the so-called Enlightening [*die Aufklärerei*] which had the impudence to boast of the authority of the letter which it alone could *interpret* was playing a false game, since the *meaning* which exegesis brings is also an understood, subjective meaning—which subjectivity of meaning was, however, at that time, the abstractions of understanding of the Wolffian school, and then later of other schools of thought, which were called reason.

Thus Hamann's Christianity is an energy of lively individual presence. In his certainty of the positive element, he remains the freest, most independent spirit, and hence at least formally open to that which seems the most remote and heterogeneous, as the examples of his reading listed above have shown. Jacobi writes in the aforementioned letter to Count Stolberg that Hamann once said: "He who cannot suffer Socrates among the prophets must be asked *who is the father of all prophets,* and whether our God did not call himself a *God of the Gentiles* [*Heiden*]."[135] He is extremely enthusiastic, at least for a few days, about *Bahrdt's* extensive systematic religion, though he knows Bahrdt to be a "heretic," since "the man speaks with light and life about love."[136] Meanwhile, Hamann's own spiritual depth lingers in completely concentrated intensity and arrives at no sort of expansion, be it in fantasy or in thought. Thought or lovely fantasy attending to a veritable content and thereby granting this expansion gives it a commonality and takes from its representation the appearance of that peculiarity which one often tends to take simply for originality. Singularity can bring forth neither any kind of work of art nor any scientific works.

Hamann's authorial character, to which we now proceed, needs no special representation or assessment, since it consists solely in the expression of the personal singularity which we have described thus far, and rarely transcends that singularity to arrive at an objective content. Our editor, in his apt characterization of Hamann's writings (R 1:viii), says that they were received upon their publication with esteem and admiration by only a few, by most rather indifferently as *unenjoyable* or even with disdain as the works of an enthusiast.[137] As for us, already Hamann's posterity, we may find both—an awareness of both respect and unenjoyability—intermingled, the unenjoyability perhaps to a greater extent for us than was the case for Hamann's contemporaries, for whom the abundance of particularities with which his works are filled could still hold more interest and also more comprehensibility than for us.

Hamann's inability to write a *book* should be self-evident by now. Our editor indicates (R 1:viii) that of Hamann's many writings, none was more than five fascicles long, most not more than two. "Further: *All* had been called into being through specific occasions, in no way undertaken of their own motivation, less so for the sake of material gain" (a few translations from the French, notices for the *Königsberger Zeitung* and other such writings, however, probably served just this purpose), "truly occasional texts, full of personality and locality, full of relation to contemporary events and experiences, but also of allusions to the literary culture in which he lived." The occasion and tendency are both polemic; reviews added the most frequent excitation of his sensitivity. What drove him to his first work, the *Socratic Memorabilia,* and what gave it its double-faced character, was, as mentioned above, on the one hand a personal cause directed toward a few people, and on the other a skewed half-directedness toward the public. The *Memorabilia* also resulted in a double critique. One came from the public in the *Hamburgische Nachrichten aus dem Reiche der Gelehrsamkeit* [*Hamburg Notices from the Realm of Scholarship*] of 1760.[138] The other was, it seems, judging by the title and the slight which Hamann felt, a bitter response from the circle of acquaintances whom Hamann had wanted to impress with his *Memorabilia;* these attacks spurred Hamann on to further pamphlets.

The *Crusades of a Philologian,* from 1762, a collection of many short, connected essays, most of them quite unimportant, but containing a few pearls,[139] brought him into contact with the *Literaturbriefe* [*Literature Letters*], with *Nicolai* and *Mendelssohn,*[140] both of whom (but especially the latter) revered his talent and sought to win him over to literary activity. In vain! Hamann would have had, in such a relation, to renounce both the singularity of his principles and the random and baroque manner of his written compositions. Instead, this relationship became the inducement for many pamphlets, both offensive and defensive, all full of individualistic wit and vengeful bitterness. He receives other agitations from other occasions, e.g., *Klopstock's* orthography,[141] the *Apology of the Freemasons* by the infamous *Starck* (who died in Darmstadt as a Catholic and a Protestant court chaplain), with whom he had earlier been in communication (see the correspondence with *Herder* and others), etc.,[142] *Eberhard's Apology of Socrates,* etc.[143] His excise office also induced him to circulate in print a few fascicles in French, among them some to Q[uintus] *Icilius,* Guichard.[144] They express his displeasure at both his meager salary and his poverty, as well as at the entire excise system and its author, *Frederick II,* and this with even more sullenness.[145] These essays brought forth no effect of any kind, either with influential individuals or with the general public. The particularity of interest and the affected, frosty humor are here far too preponderant, and there is, moreover, no evidence of any other content. Hamann did not join in the customary admiration which his countrymen and contemporaries bore toward his king, to whom he frequently and sarcastically referred as "Solomon du Nord."[146] Even less so did he raise himself up to understand or appreciate him. Rather, he never got beyond the sentiment of a German subordinate in the customs office, with Frenchmen as his superiors[147] and a meager salary indeed (which was subject on a few occasions to further reduction), or beyond the thinking of an abstract hatred toward the Enlightenment generally. It has further already been noted that besides the writings of those who were or became his opponents, almost every writing of his friends in particular became an impetus for his passionate, severe, and bitter essays. To be sure, he did not publish most of them—in

the edition at hand, many of them appear for the first time. He also ab-
stains from letting his friends, against whose writings he had railed, read
them, although he did communicate them via the hands of other
friends. Hamann was given the strongest agitation by Mendelssohn's famous *Jerusalem, or On Religious Power and Judaism;* his pamphlet directed
against it, *Golgotha and Sheblimini,* is without doubt the most significant
thing he ever wrote.[148]

Concerning the specification of the content of Hamann's writings,
as well as the form in which he expressed it, the following will offer more
noteworthy evidence of that which we have already described, rather than
any new characteristics. We have already seen that this content was the
deepest of religious truth, but held so concentrated that it remains quite
constricted in its breadth. It is the ingeniousness of the form that gives the
compact content its brilliance, and produces at the same time not an
exposition, but merely an expansion consisting of subjective particularities, self-important vagaries, and abstruse bantering, together with much
blustery ranting and grotesque, even farcical components, with which he
probably intended to amuse himself, but which could neither please nor
interest his friends, much less the general public.

He expresses his impression of his vocation in the following lovely
image (R 1:397): "A lily of the valley, and to smell in secret the savor of
knowledge, this will always be the pride that should glow most brightly in
man's heart and in his inner depths."[149] Just before, he had compared himself with the prophesying donkey of Bileam.[150] In a letter to Herr von
Moser (R 5:48), he explicates the previously mentioned parallel between
his vocation and that of Socrates as follows: "Socrates' calling, to trans-
plant morality from Olympia to the earth and to translate a little oracular
saying from Delphi" (self-knowledge) "into practical appearance, accords
with my own in that I have tried to profane a *higher sanctum* in an analogous manner, to make it common, to the understandable annoyance of
our *lying false prophets of the mouth.*[151] All my opuscula taken together make
up an Alcibiadean case [*Gehäus*]" (an allusion to the comparison with figures of silenes).[152] "Everyone has lingered over the *façon* of the sentence
or the plan, and no one has thought about the old relics *of Luther's Little
Catechism,* whose flavor and power is and will remain equal only to the
murder of the popes and Turks in each eon."[153] The title of his *Golgotha and
Sheblimini* attests to the same (R 7:125–28). The former, he explains, is
the hill on which the wood of the cross, the banner of Christianity, was
planted; what *Sheblimini* means, incidentally, one also learns here. It is, he
says, a Kabalistic name, which "*Luther,* the German Elijah and renewer of
our Christianity, which had been distorted by the liturgical and seasonal
vestments of Babylonian Baal," had given "to the *protector spirit* of his Re-

formation." "[Golgotha and Sheblimini were thus] pure silhouettes of *Christianity* and *Lutheranism* . . . who, like the cherubim, at either end of the mercy seat, shrouded the *hidden* witness of my authorship and its ark of the covenant from the eyes of the *Samaritans,* the *Philistines,* and the *mad rabble at Sichem.*"[154] To express this sort of Christianity with equal parts deep intimacy and brilliant, spirited energy, and to affirm it against Enlightenment thinkers, this is the genuine content of Hamann's writings. In all of the above, one is struck by the lack of "*façon,*" which has more or less "hidden" his purpose, i.e., does not allow it to come to explicated or more fruitful manifestation. The following passage (from *Golgotha and Sheblimini,* R 7:58) summarizes the particularity of his Christianity most decidedly: "*Unbelief* in the most real *historical* sense of the word is the only sin against the spirit of true religion, *whose heart is in heaven* and *whose heaven is in the heart.* The mystery of Christian godliness consists not in service, offerings, and vows *which God demands of humans,* but rather in promises, fulfillments, and sacrifices which God has *performed* and *accomplished* for the good of humans; not in the *loftiest and greatest commandment* which he has *imposed,* but rather in the *highest good* which he has *bestowed;* not in *legislation* and *moral doctrines* which pertain only to human dispositions and human actions, but rather in the *execution of divine deeds, works,* and *institutions* for the salvation of the entire world. *Dogmatics* and *church law* belong only to public institutions of education and administration, and as such are subject to the *arbitrary will of the authorities.* . . . These visible, public, common institutions are neither religion nor wisdom *from above,* but rather *earthly, human,* and *devilish,* according to the influence of foreign cardinals or foreign ciceroni, poetic confessors or prosaic potbellied clerics, and according to the alternating system of statistical balance and overbalance or armed tolerance and neutrality."[155] One sees that Christianity has for Hamann only such a simple presence that neither moral teaching nor the commandment to love as a commandment, nor dogmatics, nor doctrine or belief in doctrine, nor the church are its essential determinations; instead, he takes everything relating to them to be *human, earthly,* so much so that it can even be of the devil under certain circumstances. It completely escaped Hamann that the living reality of the divine spirit does not remain in such concentration, but is rather its own expansion into a world and a creation, and is so only via the production of distinctions whose limitation, certainly, but also whose right and necessity in the life of the spirit which is finite therein, must be equally acknowledged.[156] Thus, in Hamann's writings, there can only be particular passages which have any content, especially of the sort indicated. A sampling of them would probably yield a lovely collection and would perhaps appear to be the most purposeful thing that could happen to them, in order to grant the public access to that which is truly of worth within them. But it would always be difficult to lift out passages in a manner that would purify them from the nasty elements with which Hamann's writing style is everywhere afflicted.

What is interesting to note, under the circumstances which Hamann comes to discuss, is his relationship to and his opinion of philosophy. He has to depend upon it, because the theological drive of his time is immediately connected to philosophy and, first and foremost, to Wolffian philosophy. However, his time was still so far from imagining in its religious dogma even a speculative content beyond historical organization and into its interior, to which first the church fathers and then the doctors of the Middle Ages had turned, alongside their abstract historical viewpoints, that Hamann found no impetus to such observation, certainly not from without, and even less so from within himself. The two books which primarily led Hamann to speak about philosophical matters are Mendelssohn's *Jerusalem* and Kant's *Critique of Pure Reason*. It is extraordinary to see here how a concrete idea ferments in Hamann and is turned against the divisions of reflection,[157] how he opposes them with his true purpose. Mendelssohn sends Wolffian principles of natural law out ahead of his treatise, in order to establish the relationship between religion and the state. He presents the otherwise usual differentiations between perfect and imperfect duties or obligatory and benevolent duties of conscience,[158] between actions and convictions; man is led to both through reasons, to the former by *reasons that motivate the will* [*Bewegungsgründe*], to the latter by *reasons that persuade by their truth* [*Wahrheitsgründe*].[159] The state, he says, is content in any case with dead actions, with works without spirit. But even the state cannot do without convictions. For principles to be turned into convictions and morals, here religion must help the state, and the church must become a support for bourgeois society. However, the church may not have any form of government, etc.[160] Hamann's deepseeing genius is recognizable in the fact that he rightly regards those Wolffian determinations [*Bestimmungen*] as only a display (R 7:26), "in order to enact a beggarly law of nature which is barely worth mentioning and conforms neither to the state of society nor to the matter of Judaism"! He further urges quite rightly against the aforementioned differentiations (pages 39–40) that actions without convictions and convictions without actions are a bisection of complete and living duties into two dead halves, claiming thereupon that if *reasons that motivate the will* [*Bewegungsgründe*] may no longer be *reasons that persuade by their truth* [*Wahrheitsgründe*] and *reasons that persuade by their truth* [*Wahrheitsgründe*] further do not count as *reasons that motivate the will* [*Bewegungsgründe*], then all divine and human *unity* ceases in convictions and actions, etc.[161] Fruitful as these true principles are to which Hamann holds against the divisions of understanding, still the development of these principles cannot be achieved in his work, much less the more difficult task which would nonetheless be the true interest of the undertaking: to both determine and justify, with the confirmation of the higher principles, the sphere in which the formal differentiations of so-called mandatory duties and duties of conscience, etc., must take place and have their force. That to which Hamann holds fast likely comprises the *essence* of law and morality, the *substance* of society and the state; and to make these determinations—about mandatory and imperfect duties, about action without conviction, about conviction without actions—into principles of law, of morality, of the state, only brings about that well-known formalism of previous natural law and the superficialities of an abstract state. But it is just as essential that the subordinated categories also be recognized in their position, and belief in their necessity and their worth is and remains just as impregnable. There is therefore no real effect when one claims this truth and simply rejects these categories altogether; such practice must appear as empty declamation. The fact that Hamann rejects the separation of *reasons that persuade by their truth* [*Wahrheitsgründe*] from *reasons that motivate the will* [*Bewegungsgründe*] deserves especially to be distinguished, since this also corresponds to newer ideas according to which morality and religion are based not upon truth, but rather upon feeling and subjective necessities.

The other case which we want to mention in which Hamann engages with thought occurs in the essay against Kant, the *Metacritique of the Purism of Pure Reason* (R 7:1–16)—only seven pages,[162] but quite curious. This essay has already been brought to light (by Rink in *On the History of the Metacritical Invasion*, 1800)[163] in order to document the source from which *Herder* created his now long-forgotten metacritique, which appeared with great conceit and was received with just vilification, and which, as a comparison shows, has only its title in common with Hamann's clever essay.[164] Hamann places himself in the middle of the problem of reason and presents its solution; he conceives of this solution, however, in the form of *language*. Along with Hamann's thought, we will also give further examples of his execution.

He begins by listing historical standpoints of the *purification* of philosophy, the first of which is the partly misunderstood, partly unsuccessful attempt to make reason independent of all transmission, tradition, and belief therein. The second, more transcendental purification aimed, he says, at nothing less than an independence of experience and its everyday induction.[165] The *third,* highest, and yet empirical purism, *therefore*(?!), concerns *language,* the only, first, and last organon and criterion of reason (page 6), and now he says: "*Receptivity of language* and *spontaneity of concepts!* From this doubled source of ambiguity, pure reason[166] creates all the elements of its *dogmatism* [*Rechthaberei*], *skepticism* [*Zweifelsucht*], and *criticism* [*Kunstrichterschaft*], produces, through an analysis as *arbitrary* as its synthesis of the triply *old leaven,*[167] new phenomena and meteors of the changeable horizon, establishes signs and wonders with the all-creating and destroying *mercurial magic wand* of its mouth, or the forked *goose-quill* between the three *syllogistic writing-fingers* of its Herculean fist." Hamann lashes out against metaphysics with his further assurances that it "misuses all features and figures of speech of our empirical knowledge as sheer hieroglyphics and types; it manipulates, via this learned mischief, the *honesty* of language into such a *senseless, shifty, erratic, indefinable Something* = x, that nothing remains but a *windy sough, a magical shadow play,* at best, as wise (?) *Helvetius* says,[168] the talisman and rosary of a *transcendental superstition* in *entia rationis,* their empty [wine]skins and watchwords [*Losung*]."[169] Among such expectorating, Hamann further claims that the entire *faculty to think* is based in language, even if it is "the crux of the *misunderstanding* of reason with itself." "*Sounds* and *letters* are *therefore* (!?) *pure forms* a priori, in which one encounters *nothing* which belongs to *feeling* or to the *concept* of an object, and the *true aesthetic elements* of all human knowledge and reason." Now he avows himself against the Kantian division of *sensibility* and *understanding,* which trunks of knowledge spring from *one root,* and further against a violent, unwarranted, obstinate divorce of that which nature has joined together.[170] Perhaps, Hamann adds, there is "as yet *an alchemical Tree of Diana* not only for the *knowledge* of sensibility and understanding, but also for the *elucidation* and *enhancement of mutual realms* and their *limits.*"[171] In fact, in a scientific sense, there can only be one *developed* knowledge, which Hamann calls Diana's Tree, namely such that it is at the same time the touchstone of the principles which should be heralded as the *root* of thinking reason. The indication and determination of this root can be left neither to choice and arbitrary will nor to inspiration; only its explication constitutes its content and its proof. Meanwhile, Hamann continues, "without waiting for the visit of a new . . . Lucifer, or assaulting the fig-tree of the *great goddess Diana:* the wicked *bosom-serpent* of the common *language of the people* gives us the best *metaphor* for the *hypostatic unification* of the natures of the *senses* and of *understanding,* the common exchange of idiom[172] of their powers, the *synthetic* mysteries of both *corresponding* and *conflicting* forms a priori and a posteriori, together with" (the transition to the other side, that language is also the center of the *misunderstanding* of reason with itself) "the transubstantiation of *subjective* conditions and subsumptions into *objective* predicates and attributes," and this "through the *copula* of a command or expletive," namely "to curtail boredom and to fill up the empty space in the periodic galimatias[173] *per thesin* and *antithesin*" (an allusion to the Kantian antinomies). Now he exclaims: "Oh for the *action* of a *Demosthenes*" (Hamann himself was, as we have said, of a slow tongue) "and his triune (?) energy of eloquence, or the mimic which yet shall come,[174] . . . thus would I open my reader's eyes, that he might see hosts of *intuitions* ascending to the firmament of pure *understanding,* and hosts of *concepts* descending into the deep abyss of the *most tangible sensibility,* on *a ladder* of which no sleeper dares to dream, and the progressive dance of these Mahanaim or two hosts of reason, the cryptic and exasperating chronicle of their amour and rape and the whole theogony of all giant and heroic forms of Shulamite and Muse,[175] in the mythology of light and darkness, unto the *play of form* of an old Baubo *with herself—inaudita specie solaminis,* as Saint Arnobius says[176]—as a new *immaculate virgin* who may not be the *mother of God* Saint Anselm takes her for."[177]

After thus expectorating (in a manner as grandiose as it is highly baroque) his principal indignation at the abstraction, at the *blending* of both sides of the opposition, and at the products of this blending, Hamann proceeds to a more detailed account of what constitutes, for him, the concrete principle. With a *"Therefore"* and a *"Consequently"* which have no such relationship to the foregoing, he indicates that the nature of *words* is that they belong, as visible and audible, to *sensibility* and intuition, but also, according to the *spirit* of their employment and meaning, to *understanding* and to *concepts,* and are thus both pure and empirical intuitions and pure and empirical concepts.[178] But what he further links to this seems commonly psychological at best. His judgment about critical idealism is finally this: that the ability it claims "to create the *form* of an empirical intuition with neither object nor sign *out of the pure* and empty *property* of our outer and inner *mind*" is "the Δός μοι ποῦ στῶ[179] and πρῶτον ψεῦδος,[180] the entire cornerstone of critical idealism and of its tower and lodge of pure reason." He leaves it to the reader, as he introduces transcendental philosophy in the *analogy of language,* "to unclench [*entfalten*] the *balled fist* into an *open* [*flach*] *hand.*"[181] In addition to the above, we will take another passage from a letter to Herder (R 6:183). After he had said that the transcendental chatter of Kantian critique seemed to amount in the end only to *pedantic vexation* and *idle prattle* [*Schulfüchserei und Wortkram*], and that nothing seemed easier to him than the leap from one extreme to the other, he looks to dig up

Giordano Bruno's book *De uno,* in which Bruno's *principium coincidentiae* is explained, which Hamann says has been on his mind for years without him having been able *to forget it or to understand it.* This *coincidence* always seems to him the only *sufficient grounds* for all *contradictions* and the true *process* of their *resolution* and settlement, in order to put an end to all feuds about healthy reason and pure unreason.[182] We see that the idea, the *coinciding* which constitutes the content of philosophy, and which has already been discussed above in relation to his theology as well as his character, and which he would make known by way of metaphor with language, stands before Hamann's spirit in a quite constant manner. But we see also, however, that he only made a "balled fist" and left the rest, the only part of merit for science, "to unclench it into an open hand," to the reader. For his part, Hamann did not go to the effort which, if one may put it so, God did, albeit in a higher sense, to *unfold* [*entfalten*][183] in reality the balled core of truth which he is (ancient philosophers said of God that he is a round sphere) into a system of nature, into a system of the state, of justice and morality, into a system of world history, into an open [*offnen*] hand with fingers outstretched in order to grasp and pull unto himself the human spirit which is not merely an abstruse intelligence, a dull, concentrated weaving in itself, not merely a feeling and practicing, but rather a developed [*entfaltetes*] system of intelligent organization whose formal peak is thought, i.e., the capacity, according to its nature, first to transcend the surface of divine unfolding [*Entfaltung*], or rather to enter into[184] this unfolding by way of reflection *on* it, and then to ponder this divine unfolding: an effort which is both the purpose and the express duty of thinking spirit in and of itself, since *he* put off his form as a balled sphere and made himself *revealed* God—*what he is,* this and nothing else, thereby and only thereby *revealing* the relationship of nature and the spirit.

It follows from these judgments of Hamann's about Kantian critique, from the various claims of his writings and concepts, and from his particularity in general, that the need for any scientificality, the need to become aware of the content of thought and to see this content developed and preserved in thought, to gratify thought for itself, was completely foreign to Hamann's spirit.[185] The Enlightenment which Hamann combats, this aspiring to assert thought and its freedom in all interests of spirit, like the freedom of thought (albeit only formally, at first) which Kant implemented, Hamann completely overlooks, and if he was rightly unsatisfied with the forms to which this thought led, he blusters just to say the word, speaking at large and at random, against thought and reason in general, which alone can be the true means of that conscious development [*Entfaltung*] of truth and its growth into the Tree of Diana. What is more, he must further overlook the fact that the concentration (even if it is ortho-dox) which remained for him in intensive, subjective unity corresponded in its negative result with that which he was combating, in that it regarded all further development [*Entfaltung*] of doctrines of truth and faith in them as doctrines, of moral commandments and legal duties, as inconse-quential.

Now we must also reference more closely the other elements with which the general content of Hamann's work is bedizened and rather more disfigured and obscured than embellished and clarified. The in-comprehensibility of Hamann's writings, where it is not related to the con-tent presented (which itself remains incomprehensible for many), but rather to the formulation thereof, is in and of itself unpleasant, but all the more so in that it seems to the reader to be unavoidably linked with a con-trarious impression of intentionality. One senses here that Hamann's orig-inal surliness is his inimical sentiment toward the public for which he writes. Having addressed a deep interest in the reader and thus placed himself in community with him, he strikes him immediately with a gri-mace, farce, or scolding which is not made better by his use of biblical ex-pressions, a certain derision, and self-mystification, and which destroys in a spiteful manner the sympathy which he awakens, or at least makes it more difficult, and frequently in an insurmountable way, since he tosses around and screws together baroque and disparate expressions in order to mystify the reader completely, such that only very platitudinous partic-ularities are buried beneath, where he had awakened the semblance or ex-pectation of a depth of meaning. Many of these references Hamann him-self admits he no longer understands, in response to the inquiries of friends who look to him for explanations. The review literature of the time, from the fifties and the following years of the last century, the *Ham-burgische Nachrichten, Allgemeine Deutsche Bibliothek, Literaturbriefe,* and a number of other long-forgotten, obscure periodicals and writings would have to be studied thoroughly in order to recover the meaning of many of Hamann's expressions—an even more thankless and fruitless task, since it would in most cases be unsuccessful superficially, as well. Our editor himself, having promised explanatory notes in an eighth volume (R 1:xii), must add that they will only satisfy the most modest expectations. Most or indeed all of Hamann's writings are in need of a commentary which could become thicker in volume than the writings themselves. In this regard one must agree with Mendelssohn's statement (in the *Liter-aturbriefe,* part 15, upon which Hamann comments farcically at R 2:479): "Some still overcome themselves in order to pass through the sepulchral meanderings of an underground cave, when they may experience at its end sublime and important secrets. But if one cannot hope for anything but *ideas* as a reward for one's efforts to decipher an esoteric writer, then that writer probably remains unread."[186] Hamann's correspondence provides explanations about several quite particular references, the reward of which is often simply ideas which are all too frosty. If one wishes, one could look into *velo veli Dei* (R 4:187–88) and its explanation (R 5:104),[187] or *the Mamamuschi* of the three feathers (R 4:199): the name is supposedly taken from the *Gentilhomme bourgeois* [*Bourgeois Gentleman*] of Molière, not to be understood as a *Bassa* of three horsetails, but rather a newspaper writer working for Hamann's publisher and paper miller in Trutenau.[188] Another Mamamuschi appears (R 4:132) when Hamann, in typical fashion, brings forth his affairs in a little piece, "[New] Apology for the Letter H," and explains that he (see above in his biography) served on two councils, for one month and for six months, for nothing, and could not become an honest tollhouse clerk for superior competition from invalid shoe polishers and petty thieves (Hamann's own competency in his office and execution thereof should be evident from our earlier narrative), and that he is now a schoolmaster wanting only the best for his youth, and further that this is more venerable than being a well-appointed country flayer, mare-broker, and Jordan *Mamamuschi* of *three sleepyheads* with heads for nothing but extortion. These three sleepyheads mean—whom? The three *"royal Chambers* in [the cities of] Königsberg, Gumbinnen, and Marienwerder"! Of course, Hamann had even more cause to conceal his satire from royal offices, since he was applying to them at just that time for a post.[189]

We mention here another such mystification from *Golgotha and Sheblimini*, a writing whose content probably deserved to be kept purer of such farcicality. As Hamann examines (R 7:31–33) the idea of *the social contract* which predominates in most theories of natural law and of the state, both at that time and today, and quite rightly recognizes the unsound condition arising from those theories for public life, namely the absoluteness of the arbitrary, *particular* will, he opposes to this principle the divine will which is in itself universal, and rather makes the obligation of the particular will and its subordination to laws of justice and wisdom the true relationship. Consequence takes him from the *Ich* of the particular will to the thought of the monarchic principle, but his stifled excise-existence turns it all immediately into a farce: "It would not become a Solomon . . . or a Nebuchadnezzar . . . but only a Nimrod, in the state of nature,[190] to proclaim with the force of a horned brow: 'It is granted *to me and me alone* to decide whether and how much and to whom and when . . . I am *beholden to do good*'" (he could have added himself: *to do what is right*).[191] "But if the *Ich,* even in the state of nature, is so unjust and immodest, and if every man has an equal right to *Me and Me alone*, then let us be glad of the *We of God's mercy* and thankful for the crumbs which their hunting and lap dogs, greyhounds and beardogs, leave for immature [*unmündig*][192] orphans. 'Behold, he drinks up a river and is not frightened, he trusts that he can draw up Jordan into his mouth' (Job 40:23).[193] Who dares to oblige him to throw a gratuity to the poor field laborers! Who dares to keep him from *appropriating* the *Fie! Fie! of poor sinners!*"[194] Who could have determined that, according to the explanation Hamann gives in a letter to Herder, the "Fie! Fie! of poor sinners" refers to the previously mentioned *Foigelder* of the excise officials which were collected by Frederick II into the excise coffers, a loss about which Hamann was quite sensitive, and which is mentioned quite often in his letters.[195] Goethe (*From My Life,* part 3) tells of Hamann's manner as a writer. Among his collection, he says, are a few printed fascicles in which Hamann has cited by hand in the margin the passages to which his allusions refer; should one open to them, Goethe adds, there is again an ambiguous dual light which appears to us most pleasant, *but* one must completely relinquish anything called understanding. Goethe mentions here that even he was seduced by Hamann into such a sibylline style; we know how thoroughly he moved away from that, and how he further overcame that opposition which is also mentioned between *genius* and *taste* into which he also first fell with the rather energetic parrhesia of his spirit.[196]

In the manner of this last opposition, much the agenda at that time, Mendelssohn wrote in the *Literaturbriefe* his judgment of Hamann, whose entire literary character is too conspicuous not to be understood by the more sober-minded among his contemporaries: "One recognizes the *genius* in Hamann's writings, but misses *taste* in them"[197]—a category which was otherwise indifferent and permitted, but is today more or less banned from German critique; to require taste from a writing would appear to be at least an alienating demand. Hamann himself already declares this category "a *calf* that [is] the product of an Original (probably Voltaire) and of an adulterous people."[198] Mendelssohn sees in Hamann a writer who possesses fine power of judgment, has read and digested much, shows sparks of genius, and has the kernel and force of the German language in his power, who could have become one of our best writers, but who was seduced by his *desire* to be an original and thus became one of the most *reproachable*.[199] Locked up in the particular subjectivity in which Hamann's genius could not flourish into thinking or artistic form, it could only become *humor,* and what is even less fortunate, a humor besieged by much contrariety. Humor is in itself, given its subjective nature, all too ready to pass over into smugness, subjective particularities, and trivial content if not mastered by a well-mannered, well-bred, great soul. In *Hippel*, Hamann's fellow citizen, kindred spirit, and acquaintance or perhaps friend of many years, who may inarguably be called the most excellent German humorist, humor blossoms into clever form, into a talent marked by the most individual shapes, the finest and deepest sentiments and philosophically conceived thoughts and original characters, situations, and fates.[200] Hamann's humor is rather the opposite of this *objective* humor, and the expansion which he thereby gives to his perpetually concentrated truth and uses to amuse himself cannot appeal to true taste, but only to accidental *gustus*. One hears the most disparate things about these sorts of productions. Hamann's friend Jacobi, for example, said of his "New Apology for the Letter H" that he does not know "whether we have in our language something to show which would surpass this text in profoundness, wit, and humor, in richness of individual genius concerning both content and form."[201] It will be the case that no one besides the referent is in any way stimulated by this text. *Goethe* was influenced by Hamann in their time together and experienced through him a powerful stimulation, just as many such powerful excitements have gathered in such rich minds.[202] What Goethe said here and there about Hamann, much of which has already been mentioned, means we can dispense with all further engagement with description of Hamann's character as a writer. Hamann is for many not just an interesting and engaging phenomenon, but a stronghold and fulcrum when, in their desperation at the times, they needed one. We later ones must admire him as an original of his time, but can also lament that he did not find already prepared in it a spiritual form in which his genius could have fused and produced true creations for the pleasure and satisfaction of his contemporaries and successors, or that fate did not grant him the bright and benevolent sense to cultivate himself for such objective creation.

We now leave our portrayal of Hamann's existence and influence and focus, using the materials which the collection before us provides, on the end of his life. As far as his literary career is concerned, he wanted to end it with a "flying letter" which we see printed here for the first time.[203] He had already had three fascicles printed while it was still in progress, but then felt, as he writes to Herder (R 7:312–13), that he had suddenly lapsed into such *passionate, blind,* and *deaf chatter* that he had lost the first impression of his *ideal* completely and could reproduce no trace of it.[204] The printed revision retains for the most part the manner which he indicates here; the passages in the first version which are absent from the second (which comprises three-and-a-half fascicles), our editor intends to supply in the eighth volume.[205] The immediate occasion for this letter was a review, in the sixty-third volume of the *Allgemeine Deutsche Bibliothek,* of his *Golgotha and Sheblimini;* "I must take revenge on the political Philistine F." (a cipher for the reviewer) "with a jawbone of a donkey," he writes (R 7:299).[206] In this [flying] letter, he offers complete literary notes about his writings, laments the fact that he had not convinced his old friend Mendelssohn, before his death, of the honesty of his intentions,[207] repeats primarily the ideas of his *Golgotha and Sheblimini,* and expresses most especially strongly his displeasure at the "Public German Jezebel," "the Alemannish Place of the Skull" with its "blind, sleeping Homer and his companions and lads,"[208] at "the painted life-philosophy of a mephitic she-friend of man [*Menschenfreundin*],"[209] the "theologico-politico-hypocritical leaven of a Machiavellism and Jesuitism which seethes in the innards of a fundamentally spoiled nature and society, which plays its game with the brothers of Susanna and the children of Belial of our illuminated century," etc.[210] He finds frequent occasion to say that the style of his writings is repugnant to him and that he will make an effort in the future to write differently, more calmly and more clearly,[211] but he closes this essay in the same inflated, enthusiastic, repulsive manner, with the exception of a few passages in which he expresses the formal tendency of his life and his behavior as a writer with touching sentiment and lovely fantasy. As we have mentioned, at the beginning of his career, in 1759, he expressed himself on the subject via the lovely image of a lily of the valley. In 1786, at the close of his career, he expresses its fate as follows (R 7:121–22):

> For this king [whose city is Jerusalem], whose name is as great and
> unknown as his renown, the little brook of my authorship has poured
> itself out, rejected like the waters of Siloam that flow gently. Critical grav-
> ity pursued the dry chaff and every flying page of my muse,[212] because
> the dry chaff whistled, playing, with the little children sitting in the mar-
> ketplaces, and the flying page staggered and grew dizzy with the ideal of
> a king who could boast of the greatest meekness and humility of his
> heart: Something greater than Solomon is here![213] Like a loving para-
> mour tires the willing echo with the name of his beloved, and spares no
> young tree of the garden nor forest the inscription and etching of her
> name in its pulp, thus was the memory of the most beautiful among the
> sons of men, among the enemies of the king, a Magdalene-ointment
> poured out, and it flowed like the precious oil down from Aaron's head
> into his whole beard, down onto his garment.[214] The house of Simon the
> Leper in Bethany became full of the aroma of evangelic unction; but a
> few merciful brothers and critics were indignant at the waste, and their
> noses were full of only the smell of corpses.[215]

Hamann cannot resist spoiling the great earnestness with which this description begins, and the pleasing, if self-pleasing, flirtation with which it continues, with a closing image (borrowed, like most of his other expressions, from the Bible) of waste.[216]

Among this concern with the conclusions of the one interest, the hostile and struggling agitation of his life, he longed to refresh his weary spirit in the lap of his other life-pulse, friendship, or at least finally to rest therein. The fate of this friendship can be gleaned from what follows. Although the friendly intentions between Hamann and *Herder*, one of his oldest friends, remained much as they had been, and their correspondence, in which a stilted tone is tangible quite early, continued, the messages had lost more and more of their vitality of sentiment, and the tone had rather fallen into the boredom of pious lamentation. Hamann writes to Herder from Pempelfort on September 1, 1787: "For some years now, my dull, feeble correspondence must have been to you a true mirror of my sad situation."[217] Herder, who had already grown accustomed from the beginning to acting dolefully toward Hamann (just as he behaved toward others with repulsive, arrogant, lofty melancholy—see Goethe's *From My Life*),[218] answers (October 28, 1787): "I blush at my long silence, but I can't help myself. I am now so tired as well and weary of preaching," etc. [Hamann replies:] "*All is vanity*" (a common cry in his letters), "writing and effort," etc.; "you too have tasted the tedium of life," etc.[219]

About Hamann's relationship with *Hippel* and *Scheffner*, with whom he was in quite cordial and frequent contact for many years, he writes to Jacobi (April 8, 1787; Jacobi's *Works*, vol. 4, section 3, page 330): "The gait of these people is just as strange as their tone; I myself don't know what kind of figure I imagine between them. *It seems that we love and value each other without really trusting each other.* They seem to have *found* what *I am still looking for.* With all this agonizing I feel like Sancho Panza, that I must finally calm myself with the epiphoneme: *God* understands me." *Hippel* especially is for him a miracle and a mystery; how he can go about all his business and still think of such secondary things (the continuation of his *Lives*), and how he takes up moments and powers to challenge everything: "He is mayor, police chief, supreme criminal judge—takes part in all kinds of gatherings, plants gardens, has a passion for building, collects copper and paintings, knows how to unite luxury and economy, wisdom and foolishness."[220] An interesting description of such an ingenious man full of life and spirit!

Hamann says of himself (ibid. 336) that he has no one in Königsberg with whom he can talk about his subject [*Thema*], nothing but indifference.[221] His friendship with Jacobi was therefore even more intimate, their correspondence more lively (Jacobi soon replaced the formal address to Hamann with the informal *Du* and even "Father"; but Hamann, planning to travel, writes to Jacobi: "I can only use informal address [*duzen*] face to face!" Jacobi's *Correspondence,* page 376).[222] Then there was also the friendship of Herr Franz *Buchholtz,* Baron of Wellbergen bei Münster, a young man of considerable means who held the deepest respect for Hamann and asked him to accept him as his *son,* transferred considerable sums of money to him,[223] and thus relieved Hamann's worries about the subsistence and education of his family, and made possible the trip to Westphalia of both these friends. Hamann felt the pressure of obligations which reached so far; he writes to Hartknoch,[224] who had likewise offered him money, that he is suffering under the pressure of this friend's [Buchholtz's] good deeds and is so bent and bowed thereby that he cannot load any further burden onto his shoulders if he is not to succumb to the weight. He then traces his feelings back to a *mistrust of himself,* which *ties* him all the more to *Providence* and renders him a bound servant of the only Lord and Father of man.[225] The sense of friendship between these men and Hamann removed from this act of charity the natural reciprocal embarrassment or shame which would appear under other circumstances. Not only in the bizarreness of a Jean-Jacques (J. G. Hamann signed occasionally as *Hanns Görgel*) who sent his children to a foundling house (Hamann allowed his daughters to be raised in an expensive boarding house kept by a baroness)[226] and intended to subsist upon note-writing, but also more generally, in matters of financial circumstances (as well as informal address [*Duzen*], etc.), the delicacy of the French geniuses and literati of that time (see, for example, the life of Marmontel)[227] was different than in Germany. In response to applications to his office for a holiday, Hamann received a negative answer in his first year, permission to travel for a month in his second.[228] Finally, in his third year, while he was serving under the successor of Frederick II, his petition—in which it seems, according to its resolution (see ibid. 363), he probably portrayed the superfluousness of his official activity too strongly,* not thinking that the effect would reach such lengths[229]—was followed by his forced retirement (as his post was combined with another one) with only half of his salary (one hundred fifty reichsthalers, which was soon increased to two

---

*Berlin, April 26, 1787. "That there are few (and in part useless) affairs to occupy Hamann in his current position as customs warehouse administrator in Königsberg, this has long been known to us and is further affirmed by Hamann himself in the representation he has made to us. As the superfluous posts of current excise collection are now to be retracted, according to an express command, which achieve little but can be combined with others, thus," etc.

hundred). Dejected by that resolution, which Jacobi calls a "tyrant's judgment,"[230] facing the "inability to support himself and his children very
long without squandering irresponsibly the good deeds of his Buchholtz"
(capital set aside by him for the education of Hamann's children), he
made another presentation at the ministry,[231] departed in quite affected
health for Westphalia and arrived on July 16, 1787, in Münster at the home
of Fr[anz] Buchholtz, where he lived (alternately also in Jacobi's home in
Pempelfort)[232] in the bosom of intimate friendship, filled with hope that
the imminent profit of his pilgrimage, as he writes to Reichardt (R 7:362),
would be the restoration of his health and a new heart freed to the enjoy-
ment of pleasure and of life.[233]

Indeed, he found himself in a most excellent circle of quite noble,
educated, and clever people, by whom he was as beloved as esteemed
and respected, and who cared for him conscientiously—the company of
his *Jonathan* Jacobi and Jacobi's noble sisters, his *son Alcibiades* Buchholtz, his *Diotima* Princess Gallitzin, and his *Pericles* von Fürstenberg,[234]
his own eldest son, and his old friend the physician [G. I.] Lindner. As
much as reciprocal respect and love and equality in the reason of opinions surrounded this fine circle, it lay nonetheless in the manner and
constitution of friendship itself that this circle also fell, if not into resentment, then at least into mutual incomprehensibility, and labored
about therein. And incomprehensibility is perhaps worse than resentment, in that incomprehensibility is connected to and torments with the
misunderstanding of oneself, whereas resentment may only be directed
at others. It was not the case with these friends of Hamann, as with the
previously mentioned Königsberg friends, that it could appear to him
that they loved and respected each other without truly trusting each
other. But if Hamann believed that the others had already found what
he still sought, then he rather appeared to be the one who had found
what the others sought, that which they respected and enjoyed in him
and wanted to win or to sustain for themselves. If we seek out the reason
that this joy, in which such excellent individuals found themselves together, proceeded into the unexpected consequence that they ended up
nonetheless in dissatisfaction, it probably lies in the contradiction in
which they believed and took themselves and each other to be. If dispositions, thoughts, ideas, interests, principles, beliefs, and sentiments are
communicable among humans, then in the view of this circle, the
naked, concentrated intensity of mind and faith lay *outside of* and *behind*
this concreteness of individuality. This deepest and simplest thing alone
was to bear absolute value and was to be found, known, and enjoyed only
through the living presence of a confident intimacy which gave itself
completely and held nothing back. Those who fixed such separation in

their minds and tied to it their concept of beauty and even magnificence of the soul cannot satisfy each other with thoughts and deeds, with the objectivity of disposition, faith, sentiments. But the inside is only revealed, shown, communicated in that manner of sentiments, ideas, thoughts, deeds, etc. Now since in such communicating the differences and particularities of viewpoints come forth into ambiguity—for the entire situation is ambiguity itself—just as the appearance as such does not correspond to that inwardness so sought after, so demanded, so seemingly *unutterable,* and the soul [*Psyche*] itself does not give itself to understanding as such, the result is then *indéfinissable,* an incomprehensibility and unsatisfied longing, a mood in which people, without really being able to say why, find themselves separated and estranged from each other, instead of having found each other, as they believed—situations and results which Jacobi described.[235]

We will now compile the particulars as to how the actors in this novel of friendship, so to speak, are described.

Hamann writes about *Diotima, Princess Gallitzin,* always with the greatest respect. He describes her once (R 7:367) in a manner highly characteristic of her and of many of the excellencies in the area, in a letter to a friend in Königsberg: "How you would be taken in," he says, "by this singular woman of her gender, who is positively *ailing* with *passion* for greatness and *goodness* of heart."[236] The princess certainly would or rather *could* not have left this man, who had already found so much and could not have seemed to have long before his last step, unscathed by her well-known proselytizing, which of course could not ensnarl Hamann. It may not be a sign of such an attempt that he now, as he says, prefers to cite the Vulgate; but it probably is that he is now (following a visit to the "pious princess")[237] edified every morning by *Sailer's Prayer Book,* which he loves more fervently than *John* (i.e., Lavater) once he learns of it (see Jacobi's *Correspondence,* page 406). He says rightly that if Luther had not had the courage to become a heretic, Sailer would not have been in a position to write such a lovely prayer book (R 7:420–21). This prayer book was made notorious by the debate at that time over crypto-Catholicism, as a book which, if not so intended, had been used to deceive Protestants about the nature of Catholicism.[238] There is (R 7:404) an interesting letter from Hamann to the princess, written December 11, 1787, neither the inception nor the impetus of which is completely clear, but which reads: "Without *depending* on the principles which are based primarily on the prejudices of our age, and without *spurning* them either, since they belong *to the elements of the present world* and of our connection to it" (an extremely important and clever statement), "probably the surest . . .

ground of all peace is to . . . be content with the *pure* milk of the Gospel, and to orient oneself by the light given *by God,* not *by men,*" etc.[239] Dispositions are indicated here which cut short several elements of the princess's religiosity.

With *Fritz Jonathan,* Jacobi,[240] Hamann had entered during the latest time of their correspondence into many pronouncements and objections about his philosophical and polemical writings against Mendelssohn and those in Berlin.[241] Jacobi had placed the entire interest of his thought, spirit, and mind therein, with his extremely irritable personality. Almost all of Jacobi's assertions are disdainfully excoriated by Hamann in his manner, which is to say stimulating nothing, disentangling nothing, clearing up nothing. What Jacobi has established, almost entirely in Hamann's words, about faith, raising in the process much sensation and effect (if here and there only among weak people satisfied simply with the mere word "faith"), Hamann excoriates severely, as he does the oppositions between idealism and realism which occupy Jacobi as well in his *Hume* volume which was published around the same time, and in general. [They are,] Hamann writes to him, only *entia rationis,* wax noses, ideal. Only his differentiations between Christianity and Lutheranism are real, he says, *res facti,* living organs and instruments of the godhead and humanity. Thus, dogmatism and skepticism are for Hamann "perfectly identical" [*die vollkommenste Identität*], like nature and reason.[242] Even if Christianity and Lutheranism are wholly different concrete realities and actualities than abstract idealism and realism, and Hamann's spirit in truth stands above the oppositions between nature and reason, etc., it has been noted earlier in detail that Hamann was completely unfit for and unreceptive of any interest in thinking or in thoughts, and thus unfit for and unreceptive of the necessity of such differentiations. At worst, Jacobi's esteem for Spinoza (which really only had a negative sense), his belief that Spinoza had established the only consistent philosophy of understanding, was lost on Hamann, who succeeds, as usual, at nothing more than abusive blustering. That Jacobi carried around Spinoza, "the poor rogue of Cartesian-cabbalistic somnambulists, like a stone in the belly," that is all just "chimeras, words, and signs, *de mauvais(es) plaisanteries* of mathematical fiction for the arbitrary constructions of philosophical primers and bibles" (Jacobi's *Correspondence,* pages 349–57, etc).[243] "Words [*Verba*] are the idols of your concepts," he calls to him (ibid. 349), "just as Spinoza imagined the letter to be the master of the work," etc.[244] *Hemsterhuis,* whom Jacobi so respected, is equally suspicious for Hamann ("a Platonic mousetrap"); he perceives in him, as in Spinoza, only a numbskull [*taube Nüsse*], systems of lies, etc.[245] He (ibid. 341) admits honestly to Jacobi that his own writing is closer to his heart than Jacobi's, and that it seems to him, in its intention and content, both more important and more useful.[246] At that same time, Jacobi came into some distress with his defense of Starck, whom he actually despised, which he had undertaken among the members of the Berlin circle; he finds no better reception from Hamann of such a *political friendship,* as Hamann calls this defense.[247] Jacobi responded to this disapproval of all his literary endeavors only by appealing to his character, answering that there is no scientific artifice in him, and that it had never occurred to him to fool the public, or anyone, for that matter.[248] But certainly nothing more sensitive could have happened to him, given these many entanglements which called upon all the interests of his spirit, than Hamann's utterly disapproving explosions, which ran in any case so randomly and crosswise that they were little qualified to introduce or promote understanding. Yet all this did not weaken their intimate trust; in each other's presence, Jacobi was to find Hamann's soul, that last foundation of their friendship, and to recognize and learn to understand therein the resolution of all misunderstandings, the explanation of the riddle of spirit. But Jacobi writes to Lavater after a visit from Hamann, on November 14, 1787 (Jacobi's *Correspondence,* 1:435): "It cost me greatly to leave him" (more about this *leaving* later); "on the other hand it may be good that he was taken from me, so that I could collect myself again. *His art of living and being happy, I have not been able to fathom,* no matter how I let myself be abutted by it."* In another letter to Lavater of January 21, 1788 (ibid. 446): "You speak of *Buchholtz's* peculiarities; he is, to my mind, nothing, absolutely nothing compared to *Hamann.* I cannot tell *you,* how *Hamann* disposed me *to believe difficult things;* this man is a true πᾶν [everything, all] of rhymed and unrhymed, of light and darkness, of spiritualism and materialism." The result, that Jacobi "could not fathom Hamann's art of being happy," is not to be called a misunderstanding, but rather a lack of understanding; he is not made confused by this presence, but rather remains confused.

---

*Lavater (ibid., 438) says in his answer to this description of Hamann: "This strange mix of heaven and earth could, by the way, be used by one like us as a *treasure trove* of great thoughts." Later, when Rehberg used the expression in Hannover against Jacobi that he "had consorted with such *confused* minds as Lavater, among others," Jacobi answers (ibid., 471) in a similar manner in consideration of Lavater, that Lavater is *a luminous*(?) spirit in whose writings much is found which characterizes the man of genius, and which can be *used* perhaps most excellently by the most abstract and profound philosopher. From Hamann, Jacobi used only the sentences taken first from *Hume* about faith, not his *principium coincidentiae,* the concreteness of his idea. One may wonder at such intimate friendship being reduced to the cold end of "use."

Finally, regarding the other *son, Alcibiades Buchholtz*, whose generous gifts and trustful relationship comprised the basis of Hamann's trip, Jacobi writes of him, in addition to the aforementioned, to Lavater on July 23, 1788, after Hamann's death (ibid. 482): "Buchholtz and his wife, etc., have departed; God, how this man depressed me. I just got to know this strange person better last April, when I was in Münster to visit Hamann. The gift which he received from Buchholtz, Hamann *probably repaid with his life.* And yet, this same Buchholtz has characteristics which instill respect, admiration, and love. I don't believe that a human soul can be purer than his. *But his company kills.*"

Hamann himself was at first depressed by his bodily condition; he had departed for his trip, he writes (R 7:411), "with swollen feet and a twenty-year-old load of evil juices which I had collected through a lifestyle of sitting and brooding, of passionate immoderation in nourishment for my stomach and my mind."[249] He also speaks of this immoderation in eating and in reading during his stay in Westphalia, and that in reading is recognizable enough in his letters.[250] The spa cures, medical treatment, and most attentive and loving care which he enjoyed during his stay in Münster, Pempelfort, and Wellbergen could no longer renew his weakened body. For his part, he expresses everywhere the most complete satisfaction which he enjoyed in this new circle of associations. To be *the panegyrist* or *critic* of his charitable friends could not occur to him, however (R 7:366).[251] "I live here," he writes on March 21, 1788, from Münster, "in the bosom of friends cast from the same mold, who fit like other halves to my *ideals of the soul.* I have *found*, and am as glad of my finding as the shepherd and the woman in the Gospel; and if there is a foretaste of heaven on earth, then this treasure has not come to me out of merit or worthiness" (R 7:409).[252] He says often that the love and honor which he experiences are indescribable, and it took an effort for him to endure and explain it. He was at first "stunned and *dumbfounded* by it all."[253] He always expresses himself in this sense and [in] the sentiment of love, just as the letters to his children from this period are quite mild, attractive, and touching.[254] But Hamann, who was aware that Jacobi had endured, given Hamann's nasty moods, many difficult tests of patience and was expecting more (R 7:376),[255] Hamann, who was, with his perfect inner indifference toward everything, all the more capable of enduring, could nonetheless no longer endure it among these "ideal ones of humanity,"[256] as he frequently describes his surroundings. That so much was happening inside him which he doesn't describe, and which was not absent from the sentiment "of so indescribably much goodness and charitableness"[257] which he enjoyed, was already to be concluded from the surroundings he describes; but more determined glimpses of the same impose themselves. Jacobi tells, a few months after Hamann's death (Jacobi's *Correspondence,* 1:486), how Hamann had compared himself with one possessed, thrown by an evil spirit first into fire, then into water; this comparison would suit him (Jacobi) also in a way. "Oh, that the hand would appear to me," he cries, "which could teach me *to walk along the path of human existence.*—The hand, the hand! I called again and again to my Hamann. 'Perhaps' was, among a stream of tears, one of the last words which I heard from his mouth." One sees here two men so broken in themselves, still so in need of instruction *to walk along the path of human existence,* facing each other, having already passed through such a deeply emotional life.

After his stay for several months with Jacobi (in Pempelfort from August 12, and then in Düsseldorf from October 1 until November 5, 1787), Hamann suddenly leaves his friend's house, throws himself, without a word as to his intentions, in miserable weather and in health which he believes to be reviving, into the post-carriage, and returns to Buchholtz in Münster.[258] A specific explanation as to this flight, which he says he had to execute "with force and cunning" (a few tickets which seem relevant are not printed; see Jacobi's *Correspondence,* page 384), certainly does not lie in regrettable occurrences or injurious behaviors, but rather in the opposite, which elevated his embarrassment into fear which he only knew how to vent via flight.[259] He explains himself on this subject only as follows (Jacobi's *Correspondence,* page 386): "You, poor Jonathan, have done us wrong, your two sisters and me, Lazarus,[260] in burdening their sex, which nature made softer and tamer, with the hard yoke and the heavy burden of such a *masculine* friendship, such a *holy* landscape as that which presides over us. Have you not noticed, dear Jonathan, that these two *Amazons* made it a point to deprive me, poor old man, of the honor of my whole philosophy, of all of your favorable judgments thereof, and to bring us both into such embarrassment that we would seem ridiculous to each other and even to ourselves, like a couple of *philosophical ghosts?*"[261] Hamann's philosophizing, or whatever one wants to call the will-o'-the-wisp ghostliness of his feeling and consciousness, could easily develop, among clever ladies (with whom one could not get by with the blustering and crudities with which he served himself), into feelings of affliction and fear, when solicited to step out of its nebulousness to the clarity of thought or sentiment. The next letter from Hamann reads: "The love which I enjoyed in your house bears no relationship to my merit; I have been taken up into it *like an angel of heaven.* Had I been an *incarnate son of Zeus* or *Hermes,* I could not have found a greater sacrifice of hospitality and generous self-denial than that in which Helene" (one of Jacobi's sisters) "has immortally distinguished herself. Should I now attribute this *exaggeration* of *sympathy* simply to my needs rather than to friendship for me, and somehow arrogate that which belonged more to you than to me?"[262] The extreme respect and attentiveness which he enjoyed and which he attributed to his friendship for Jacobi and not to his personality, only increased his embarrassment and the difficulty of his condition.[263]

In the same letter (of November 17, 1787;[264] see Jacobi's *Correspondence*, page 383), Hamann appeals, on account of his flight, to Jacobi's friendship, as the Jonathan of his soul which he is and will remain as long as he (Hamann) is conscious of his existence and his life, after so many important obligations for all the good, etc. To Jacobi's inquiry, whether he (Hamann) was doing poorly during his stay with Buchholtz in Münster, Hamann replied: "Here, in the true place of my destiny and my departure from my fatherland? Wasn't it my Franz (Buchholtz) who called me and outfitted me for this whole life, which I live in the best hopes and with the fullest intention of passing away with peace and joy? Here I should be doing poorly, where I am like a fish and a bird in my proper element?"[265] This sentiment and opinion notwithstanding, Hamann could not endure it for long, even there. Jacobi writes on January 21, 1788, to Lavater: "Hamann was in Münster hardly fourteen days before he had the idea to travel all alone to Wellbergen, to Buchholtz's estate. No remonstrances, pleas, or crossness could help; he left. And what all had predicted occurred; he fell ill" (Jacobi's *Correspondence*, 1:446). After a three-month stay that winter at that place which Jacobi calls a damp morass, during which the correspondence between them stagnated, Hamann returned to Münster toward the end of March, and intended after the middle of June to visit Jacobi once more, in order to bid him farewell and to return to Prussia.[266] But on the designated day of departure he became seriously ill, and the following day, June 21, 1788, saw the peaceful and painless end of his besieged life.

Appendix: Hegel's Notebook Entries on Hamann

Hamann—drama or novel.

The novel represents for us the position of the drama—since [man today] must settle [the] conflict of the characters within himself.

Reconciliation with oneself—[one is] more complete [*fertiger*] in *his* way—decline—character can be understood as facility [*Fertigkeit*], reconciliation, or as decline.

Decline into a philistine's life—giving up the difficult tears of passion's ideal. Hamann walked through not ideals, resolutions of youth—not generality, ideals announced themselves in him—not an outlook on art. Immediately aimed at particular individualities—their improvement, rectification. Not the poetry of youth—

Stuck, so to speak, in friendship, i.e., direction toward detail. Polemics—not of the ideal against reality.

Germans [are] not, never at home in themselves—from the beginning of their history—raids—migrations—honestly—i.e., positive habit—and theoretically—extravagance—not character.

Modern times—descriptions—differences in manner, being outside oneself, i.e., being crazy.

Hamann's Kant critique, R 6:183, 186–87. Another germ of later, higher self-education from the inside out, whose time is to awaken in youth, is not distinguishable in Hamann—a poetry of youth, a fantasizing, passion, if you will—an interest which is certainly still quite ideal, general, immature, but firm, passion for an object of intellectual activity, science, which becomes decisive in his life.

Hamann not in this torture of the Pietists—sinning, doing penance—but [one] feels no sins. Torturing [oneself], believing oneself a sinner—the sublime, the highest grief, not to recognize his sins; see Hahn[1]—the *self-conceit,* to make oneself lamentingly a sinner, lying to oneself, to be a sinner, that one is a sinner, and the grace of God—Hamann was really a sinner; bad jokes.

Translator's Notes

Introduction

1. For the relationship between Hegel and Roth, see Karlfried Gründer, "Nachspiel zu Hegels Hamann-Rezension," *Hegel-Studien* 1 (1961): 89.

2. For Hegel's seminal role in the history of this serial, see G. W. F. Hegel, *Werke*, ed. Eva Moldenhauer and Karl Markus Michel (Frankfurt: Suhrkamp, 1969–71), 11:579.

3. Sossio Giametta, *Hamann nella considerazione di Hegel, Goethe, Croce: In appendice due scritti di Hegel su Hamann* (Naples: Bibliopolis, 1984); Jacques Colette, trans. and ed., *Hegel: Les écrits de Hamann* (Paris: Éditions Aubier-Montaigne, 1981); Pierre Klossowski, *Les Méditations Bibliques de Hamann. Avec une étude de Hegel* (Paris: Éditions de Minuit, 1948).

4. For Hamann's biography in English, see James C. O'Flaherty, *Johann Georg Hamann* (Boston: Twayne, 1979).

5. Gwen Griffith Dickson, *Johann Georg Hamann's Relational Metacriticism* (New York: De Gruyter, 1995).

6. Hegel begins his review of F. H. Jacobi's works, by contrast, by remarking that while he is full of personal respect for Jacobi, he does not feel it appropriate to comment on Jacobi the man, and will confine himself to Jacobi's literary production (G. W. F. Hegel, *Werke: Vollständige Ausgabe durch einen Verein von Freunden des Verewigten,* ed. Philipp Marheineke et al. [Berlin: Duncker und Humblot, 1832–45], 16:203).

7. Isaiah Berlin, *The Magus of the North: J. G. Hamann and the Origins of Modern Irrationalism* (New York: Farrar, Straus and Giroux, 1993), 4.

8. Dickson, *Hamann's Relational Metacriticism*, 325.

9. Ibid.

10. Josef Nadler, *Johann Georg Hamann: Der Zeuge des Corpus mysticum* (Salzburg: Otto Müller, 1949), 483.

11. Stephen Dunning, *The Tongues of Men: Hegel and Hamann on Religious Language and History* (Missoula: Scholars Press, 1979), 28. The fourth chapter of Dunning's book is concerned entirely with Hegel's essay.

12. Eric Achermann, *Worte und Werte: Geld und Sprache bei Gottfried Wilhelm Leibniz, Johann Georg Hamann und Adam Müller* (Tübingen: Niemeyer, 1997), 55.

13. G. W. F. Hegel, *Lectures on the Philosophy of Religion*, ed. Peter C. Hodgson, trans. R. F. Brown et al. (Berkeley: University of California Press, 1984–87), 1:167.

14. Hegel is adapting here the image that Hamann has borrowed—the balled fist/open hand—from the Stoic philosopher Zeno of Citium. See R 7:16, N 3:289, and Oswald Bayer, *Vernunft ist Sprache: Hamanns Metakritik Kants* (Stuttgart: Frommann-Holzboog, 2002), 418–19.

15. Dunning, *Tongues of Men*, 35.

16. Manfred Kuehn, *Kant: A Biography* (New York: Cambridge University Press, 2001), 119–20.

The Notion of Friendship in Hegel and Hamann

1. Dickson, *Hamann's Relational Metacriticism*, 24.

2. James C. O'Flaherty, trans. and ed., *Socratic Memorabilia: A Translation and Commentary* (Baltimore: Johns Hopkins University Press, 1967), 33.

3. Nadler, *Johann Georg Hamann*, 38.

4. Karlfried Gründer, "Hamann in Münster," in *Johann Georg Hamann*, ed. Reiner Wild (Darmstadt: Wissenschaftliche Buchgesellschaft, 1978), 271.

5. For a recent commentary on the eighteenth century as the "century of friendship" in Germany, see Jost Hermand, *Freundschaft: Zur Geschichte einer sozialen Bindung* (Cologne: Böhlau, 2006), 11.

6. Nadler, *Johann Georg Hamann*, 300.

7. See Kuehn, *Kant: A Biography*, 165.

8. See *HH*, 23 and 46.

9. In his recent book on friendship in the German tradition, Hermand summarizes quite well this connection in the context of the Pietism of Hamann's time, "which saw the essence of Christianity above all in highly personal experience of sentiment, thus establishing a new ethic of love and friendship within orthodoxly sclerotic Protestantism" (Hermand, *Freundschaft*, 16).

10. Diane Morgan, "Amical Treachery: Kant, Hamann, Derrida and the Politics of Friendship," *Angelaki: Journal of the Theoretical Humanities* 3, no. 3 (1998): 145. Kant offers a related analysis of friendship throughout his essay "On a Supposed Right to Lie from Philanthropy." Here he acknowledges that the friend is "in constant danger of losing something of his friend's respect, since he is observed and secretly criticized by him; and even the fact that he is observed and mastered will seem in itself offensive" (Immanuel Kant, *Practical Philosophy*, ed. Allen Wood, trans. Mary Gregor [Cambridge: Cambridge University Press, 1996], 585). In Hamann's case, the criticism was not so secret, and he seems to have assumed, at least early in life and considerably more naively than Kant, that his friends would accept it without any real or lasting loss of respect on either side. Peter Fenves's analysis of Kant's text, though it does not refer to Hamann, is particularly relevant. See Peter Fenves, "Politics of Friendship—Once Again," *Eighteenth-Century Studies* 32, no. 2 (1998–99): 136–40.

11. Quoted and translated in Kuehn, *Kant: A Biography*, 170.

12. Much has been written about the meeting which took place between Hegel and Goethe in 1827, and the fact that much of their conversation centered

around Hamann. For the original narration of the meeting, see W. F. von Biedermann, *Goethes Gespräche* (Leipzig: Biedermann, 1909–11), 3:477.

13. Johann Wolfgang von Goethe, *From My Life: Poetry and Truth: Parts One to Three*, ed. Thomas P. Saine and Jeffrey L. Sammons, trans. Robert R. Heitner (New York: Suhrkamp, 1994), 381–82. All translations of Goethe in this volume are Robert R. Heitner's.

14. Hermand, *Freundschaft*, 16. See also Wolfdietrich Rasch, *Freundschaftskult und Freundschaftsbildung im deutschen Schrifttum des 18. Jahrhunderts* (Halle: Niemeyer, 1936), 46. (For an important situation of Rasch's work among the German literature on friendship, see Fenves, "Politics of Friendship," note 9.)

15. See also *HH*, 42, for Goethe and parrhesia.

16. Michel Foucault, *Fearless Speech*, ed. Joseph Pearson (Los Angeles: Semiotext(e), 2001), 12, 14, 106.

17. Fenves, "Politics of Friendship," 140.

18. See Foucault, *Fearless Speech*, 16, where he insists that risk is a part of parrhesiastic speech, and specifies the risk of losing a friend's affection as a common example.

19. John McCumber, "Hegel and Hamann: Ideas and Life," in *Hegel and the Tradition*, ed. Michael Baur and John Russon (Toronto: University of Toronto Press, 1997), 78.

20. Foucault, *Fearless Speech*, 24, 106.

21. James C. O'Flaherty, *The Quarrel of Reason with Itself: Essays on Hamann, Nietzsche, Lessing and Michaelis* (Columbia: Camden House, 1988), 41.

22. For Socrates as a prophet in Hamann's thought, see *HH*, 20 and 31.

23. See John R. Betz, "Enlightenment Revisited: Hamann as the First and Best Critic of Kant's Philosophy," *Modern Theology* 20, no. 2 (2004): 294.

24. See O'Flaherty, *Quarrel of Reason*, 52–54.

25. Hamann had previously written translations, as well as his *Biblical Meditations* and *Thoughts About My Life*, texts originally intended only for his relatives and close friends.

26. Interestingly, this development comes full circle later in Hamann's life. McCumber points out, following Hegel, that when Hamann's "reduction of Christianity"—and many other things, as Hegel would undoubtedly argue—"to his own rhapsodies" "deprived him . . . of a public," "this meant that he relied greatly on his private circle: on his friends" (McCumber, "Hegel and Hamann," 78).

27. See *HH*, 19.

28. See Betz, "Enlightenment Revisited," 295.

29. Translated and annotated by Garrett Green in James B. Schmidt, ed., *What Is Enlightenment? Eighteenth-Century Answers and Twentieth-Century Questions* (Berkeley: University of California Press, 1996), 145–53.

30. Translated and annotated by Kenneth Haynes in Schmidt, *What Is Enlightenment?* 154–67. This translation is reprinted in Johann Georg Hamann, *Writings on Philosophy and Language*, trans. and ed. Kenneth Haynes (Cambridge: Cambridge University Press, 2007), 205–18. See also Bayer, *Vernunft ist Sprache*.

31. Berlin, *Magus of the North*, 109.

32. O'Flaherty, *Socratic Memorabilia*, 33.

33. Kuehn, *Kant: A Biography,* 323. Josef Simon observes that what we know of the relationship between these two men comes almost exclusively from Hamann's side, relatively few public comments about Hamann having come from Kant (Josef Simon, "Spuren Hamanns bei Kant?" in *Hamann—Kant—Herder: Acta des vierten Internationalen Hamann-Kolloquiums im Herder-Institut zu Marburg/Lahn 1985* [Frankfurt: Peter Lang, 1987], 89).

34. Morgan, "Amical Treachery," 148.

35. Fenves, "Politics of Friendship," 147. See also Jacques Derrida, *The Politics of Friendship,* trans. George Collins (London: Verso, 2005), 29.

36. Quoted in Karl Rosenkranz, "Hamann und Kant: Eine Parallele," in *Johann Georg Hamann,* ed. Wild, 20.

37. Herder would not be Hamann's last Alcibiades; he would later use the same nickname for Buchholtz, who provided sorely needed financial assistance and asked Hamann to take him on as a son. Hamann willingly did so. See R 7:168, 184; ZH 5:218, 283.

38. Nadler, *Johann Georg Hamann,* 150, 365.

39. Ibid., 150. See also R 5:10; ZH 3:12.

40. Nadler, *Johann Georg Hamann,* 153.

41. See Renate Knoll, *Johann Georg Hamann und Friedrich Heinrich Jacobi* (Heidelberg: Winter, 1963), 23.

42. Ibid., 68.

43. Nadler, *Johann Georg Hamann,* 365.

44. Ibid., 366.

45. Ibid., 367.

46. See *HH,* 35–39.

47. See Knoll, *Johann Georg Hamann,* 99.

48. Hegel later points out that Hamann "did not publish most of" these "passionate, severe, and bitter essays," so that "many of them appear for the first time" (*HH,* 32–33) in the Roth edition which Hegel is reviewing.

49. See *HH,* 46.

50. Hamann wrote similarly to Johann Gottfried Herder: "Isn't it the same in friendship as in love? Both are the ruination of so many people, and turn from the most precious wine into vinegar" (R 6:172; ZH 4:257). And he writes in the *Socratic Memorabilia,* in defense of Socrates' homosexuality, that one "cannot feel a lively friendship without sensuality" (R 2:25; N 2:68).

51. For the relationship between marriage, friendship, and family in the eighteenth century, see Bengt Algot Sørensen, "Freundschaft und Patriarchat im 18. Jahrhundert," in *Frauenfreundschaft—Männerfreundschaft: Literarische Diskurse im 18. Jahrhundert,* ed. Wolfram Mauser and Barbara Becker-Cantarino (Tübingen: Niemeyer, 1991), 279–92.

52. Nadler, *Johann Georg Hamann,* 304. For the tenuous place of women in the *Freundschaftskult* of Hamann's time, as well as a review of more recent scholarship about it, see Magdalene Heuser, "'Das beständige Angedencken vertritt die Stelle der Gegenwart': Frauen und Freundschaften in Briefen der Frühaufklärung und Empfindsamkeit," in *Frauenfreundschaft—Männerfreundschaft,* ed. Mauser and Becker-Cantarino, 141–45.

53. Stolberg and his brother were also part of the Göttinger Hain circle, one of the most famous embodiments of the eighteenth century's ideals of literary friendship.

54. Goethe also joined this circle from time to time, although not while Hamann was there. See Gründer, "Hamann in Münster," 280.

55. Ibid., 272.

56. Ibid., 286.

57. G. W. F. Hegel, *The Phenomenology of Mind,* trans. and ed. J. B. Baillie, 2nd ed. (New York: Humanities, 1977), 675–76.

58. Hegel, *Lectures on the Philosophy of Religion,* 3:285–86.

59. McCumber, "Hegel and Hamann," 77–78.

60. Ibid., 78.

61. Wolfram Mauser and Barbara Becker-Cantarino, "Vorwort," in *Frauen-freundschaft—Männerfreundschaft,* ed. Mauser and Becker-Cantarino, vii.

62. Fenves, "Politics of Friendship," 133. See also Friedrich Vollhardt, "Freundschaft und Pflicht: Naturrechtliches Denken und literarisches Freundschaftsideal im 18. Jahrhundert," in *Frauenfreundschaft—Männerfreundschaft,* ed. Mauser and Becker-Cantarino, 293–309.

63. Aristotle, *The Nicomachean Ethics,* trans. David Ross (Oxford: Oxford University Press, 1980), 192.

64. Ibid.

The Writings of Hamann

1. Goethe notes in his autobiography that he "possess[es] an almost complete collection of [Hamann's] writings," and further establishes there his (ultimately unrealized) intention to do one day what Hegel does in the essay at hand: "I still hope either to do an edition of Hamann's works myself or at least to promote one, and then, when these important documents are again brought before the public, it might be time to discuss details of the author's nature and character" (Goethe, *From My Life,* 380).

2. Prussian statesman Georg Heinrich Ludwig Nicolovius (1767–1839).

3. This correspondence between Hamann and Jacobi can be referenced only from Jacobi's *Exquisite Correspondence* (*Auserlesener Briefwechsel,* ed. Friedrich Roth [Leipzig: Fleischer, 1825–27]), which Hegel will use, and from the ZH edition of Hamann's letters, as in subsequent notes. Hegel's previous review of Jacobi's works (in two parts, 1813 and 1817) may also be of interest.

4. This eighth volume of the Roth edition was published in 1842 and 1843, in two parts, so that Hegel never saw it.

5. The *Allgemeine Deutsche Bibliothek* was a key scholarly journal of the German Enlightenment in which major publications of the time were reviewed. It was edited by Friedrich Nicolai in Berlin from 1765 to 1796.

6. Goethe writes of the "aspiring younger generation [which] found itself strongly attracted to" Hamann (Goethe, *From My Life,* 379).

7. It seems this nickname was coined by the statesman Karl Friedrich von

Moser (1723–98), who used it to indicate that Hamann had, like the Magi, seen the Star of Bethlehem (see Matthew 2:2). See O'Flaherty, *Socratic Memorabilia*, 4; Ronald Gregor Smith, *J. G. Hamann: A Study in Christian Existence, with Selections from His Writings* (New York: Harper, 1960), 22. Hamann accepted the nickname and often used it, especially in his writings, to refer to himself.

8. Friedrich Nicolai (1733–1811) and Moses Mendelssohn (1729–86) were at the center of the Berlin Enlightenment. Less well known for their contributions to the German Enlightenment are the Protestant theologians Hegel mentions: Wilhelm Abraham Teller (1734–1804), Johann Joachim Spalding (1714–1804), Gotthelf Samuel Steinbart (1738–1809), and Johann Friedrich Wilhelm Jerusalem (1709–89). Hegel also refers to the scholar Johann Friedrich Zöllner (1753–1804) and the prolific philosopher Johann August Eberhard (1739–1809).

9. See R 3:191; ZH 2:203.

10. See McCumber, "Hegel and Hamann," 77, on Kant's principles of enlarged thought.

11. N 2:9–54.

12. R 1:51–53; N 1:7–8. For God as a pillar of cloud or fire, see Exodus 13:21–22.

13. Johann Christoph Hamann (1697–1766). Johann Georg was named after his uncle (1697–1733), who was himself a well-known author. This uncle wrote the second part of the novel *Die asiatische Banise* and compiled a widely used poetic lexicon. Many of his hymns were set to music, some in collaboration with Händel.

14. N 2:11–12. Hamann's brother Johann Christoph was two years younger than he.

15. Donatus was a Roman grammarian and rhetorician; his work presents the first rules of Latin grammar.

16. R 1:155–56; N 2:12–13.

17. Johann Bernhard Basedow (1723–90) and Joachim Heinrich Campe (1746–1818) were two pedagogical reformers of the German Enlightenment.

18. R 1:157–58; N 2:14.

19. R 1:157; N 2:13–14.

20. R 1:163; N 2:16–17. The reference is to Matthew 13:25.

21. R 1:168–72; N 2:19–21. Where Hegel has "euphonic" (*wohllautenden*), Hamann actually writes "full-sounding" (*vollautenden*).

22. R 1:173; N 2:21–22.

23. N 2:23.

24. R 1:177; N 2:23–24. Hamann's pupil was Woldemar Dietrich von Budberg (1740–84), son of Baroness Barbara Helena von Budberg (1716–81).

25. At the estate of Count von Witten in Courland.

26. R 1:186; N 2:28.

27. Hamann befriended Johann Christoph Berens (1729–92) at university.

28. R 1:182; N 2:26.

29. R 1:184–85; N 2:27.

30. R 1:187; N 2:28.

31. N 2:29.

32. R 1:188–95; N 2:29–32. The "others" Hamann met in Berlin were Johann

Georg Sulzer (1720–79), best known for his *Common Theory of the Fine Arts* (1771–74), and the poet Karl Wilhelm Ramler (1725–98). See O'Flaherty, *Socratic Memorabilia,* 29. Hamann's mother, Maria Magdalene (née Nuppenau), was a native of Lübeck.

33. R 1:196–200; N 2:32–34.

34. This is probably at least partly speculation on Hegel's part. Hamann scholars have not been able to ascertain with certainty the nature of the business on which the Berens family sent Hamann to London. It is clear that the trip was either intended as or at least became a sort of *Bildungsreise* that determined the rest of Hamann's life, as Hegel will soon detail. But the initial nature of the mission remains largely unclear.

35. R 1:200–202; N 2:34–36.

36. R 1:207–8; N 2:38–39.

37. R 1:211–13; N 2:40–41.

38. R 1:214–15; N 2:41–42. The Hamann text from which Hegel excerpts reads as follows: "My sins are debts of infinitely greater importance and consequence than my temporal ones. To gain the whole world would not pay the former; and if Abraham had to hear Ephron because of a Canaanite and give him 400 shekels of silver: what is that between you and me? Should God not allow a Christian to think more nobly than a pagan? As the former is made right in him, in the main sense, then how should it matter to God that a trifle be offered up in addition?" For the first reference, see Matthew 16:26, Mark 8:36, and Luke 9:25; for the second, see Genesis 23:15–16.

39. The title page of *Thoughts About My Life* includes the date April 21, 1758. The lengthy first section which Hegel has finished reviewing ends with the date April 24, 1758. The sections which follow are dated somewhat sporadically.

40. R 1:227–38; N 2:48–53. The woman in question is Katharina Berens (1727–1805).

41. N 2:53. Hegel mistakenly has the page number in the Roth edition as 230. The question mark in the text, like all of those which follow, is Hegel's. For the biblical reference, see 2 Kings 19:3.

42. R 1:337; ZH 1:287.

43. R 1:241–42; N 2:54.

44. Arend Berens (1723–67). R 1:337; ZH 1:287.

45. Hamann and Berens had likewise befriended Johann Gotthelf Lindner (1729–76) at university. Hamann calls this friendship a "triumvirate" in which "friendship seethed in all three of us equally strongly. We burned to see and to enjoy each other" (R 1:183; N 2:26).

46. ZH 1:308, 304.

47. R 1:369–71; ZH 1:315–16. Hegel seems to have confused the names here, as Herodias is the mother, not the daughter, in the well-known story. See Matthew 14:1–12; Mark 6:17–29.

48. R 1:440; ZH 1:378. Alexander Gottlieb Baumgarten (1714–62) was a German philosopher in the tradition of Leibniz and Wolff. His seminal study of aesthetics was especially formative for Hamann. This entire letter is quite famous for Hamann's rejection of Kantian rationalism.

49. R 1:429; ZH 1:373.

50. R 1:506–8; ZH 1:449–50.

51. R 1:392–95; ZH 1:339–41. See 1 Timothy 1:15; Genesis 37.

52. R 1:363–64; ZH 1:309.

53. Hegel quotes here from a letter Hamann wrote to Lindner on March 21, 1759 (R 1:360; ZH 1:307). Hamann mistakenly refers to the words uttered by Martin Luther in Worms (not Augsburg) in 1521.

54. ZH 1:380, 2:11.

55. R 1:357–60; ZH 1:306–7.

56. See Luke 18:34.

57. R 1:484–86; ZH 1:413–16.

58. R 1:441; ZH 1:379. The reference to the tree known by its fruits is from Matthew 7:15–20. It is also a key theme in Martin Luther's "On Christian Freedom," which Hamann would have known well.

59. R 1:395; ZH 1:341.

60. ZH 1:448.

61. 1 Corinthians 11:32.

62. ZH 1:321, 303, 339. The quotation references 2 Corinthians 7:12.

63. ZH 1:448–53, 399, 430. Hegel mistakenly cites page 405, not 495, of the Roth edition for the final reference.

64. After Hamann's letter to Lindner of November 7, 1759, there is a break in the correspondence until April 12, 1760, after which Hamann's letters to Lindner become quite frequent again. See ZH vols. 1 and 2.

65. R 7:73; N 3:349.

66. R 1:429–30; ZH 1:373.

67. ZH 1:377.

68. ZH 1:448–49.

69. R 3:309; ZH 2:231.

70. R 2:1; N 2:57. Hegel paraphrases Hamann's dedications here. For Hamann's feelings about "the public," see Haynes's introduction to Hamann's *Writings on Philosophy and Language*, viii–ix.

71. N 2:59–60. Kant defines the *Menschenfreund* as "one who takes an affective interest in the well-being of all human beings," and insists that this is not quite the same thing as "a philanthropist" (Kant, *Practical Philosophy*, 587). For further analysis of this term in its eighteenth-century context, see Felicitas Munzel, "Menschenfreundschaft: Friendship and Pedagogy in Kant," *Eighteenth-Century Studies* 32, no. 2 (1998–99): 247–59. The "philosopher's stone" refers to the *lapis philosophorum* with which alchemists attempted to turn metal into gold. Hamann often compares the philosophers of his age with alchemists, and he later refers to this stone again (see R 4:196; N 3:131), especially in his metacritique of Kant (R 7:5; N 3:284). Here in the *Memorabilia*, the image seems a criticism of Berens's interest not only in philosophy but in betterment via monetary gain as well. The reference to Newton and his position at the mint, in connection with Kant (whom Hamann identifies as a Newtonian elsewhere, as well), allows Hamann to draw a parallel between the appraisal of coins and critique; he goes on to juxtapose con-

version rates for money with the weightiness of ideas. See also O'Flaherty, *Socratic Memorabilia*, 190; and Dickson, *Hamann's Relational Metacriticism*, 35–36.

72. R 2:31–35; N 2:71–73. The Hamann text reads as follows: "But Socrates exceeded them both [Sophocles and Euripides] in wisdom, since he had come farther in self-knowledge than they and knew that he knew nothing." Hegel then skips over, without indicating it, a number of paragraphs of the *Memorabilia*, and picks up with his paraphrase where Hamann writes: "When Socrates gives Crito account with his *I know nothing!*, when he turned away the learned and curious Athenians with just these words, and tried to facilitate for his lovely lads the disavowal of their vanity and to gain their trust through his equality with them . . . ." Hegel again skips over a paragraph's worth of text, beginning again roughly where Hamann resumes: ". . . when he [Socrates] said to the Sophists, to the scholars of his time: I know nothing. Thus it was that this sentence was a thorn in their eyes and a lashing on their backs. All of Socrates' *ideas,* which were nothing but *emissions* and *secretions* of his *ignorance,* seemed to them as appalling as the hair on the head of Medusa, the navel of the aegis." While the aegis of Zeus is routinely described as "awful to behold," I have not been able to trace the reference specifically to its navel. See Edith Hamilton, *Mythology* (Boston: Little, Brown, 1942), 26.

73. R 2:35–36; N 2:73–74. See Psalm 34:8.

74. R 2:37–38; N 2:74. The actual reference is 1 Corinthians 8:2–3; the error seems to be Hegel's.

75. R 2:39–40; N 2:75–76.

76. R 2:48–49; N 2:81. Hamann includes the explicit reference to Matthew in his text.

77. For the relationship between faith, being, and existence in Hamann, see R 4:326–30; N 3:190–92.

78. This and the following four paragraphs are not present in the 1832–45 edition of Hegel's works, likely because Hamann's daughter took offense at them. (See Gründer, "Nachspiel zu Hegels Hamann-Rezension," 89–91.) I am grateful to the Felix Meiner Verlag for their permission to reprint these paragraphs here.

79. R 5:58; ZH 3:72.

80. Hamann's common-law wife was Anna Regina Schumacher (1736–89), who began employment as a housekeeper in Hamann's father's house in 1762. Their children were Johann Michael Hamann (born 1769), Elisabeth Regina Hamann (born 1772), Magdalena Katharina Hamann (born 1774), and Marianne Sophie Hamann (born 1778).

81. N 2:52. Hegel leaves out the words after "give me no other," namely, "than the sister of my friend" (Katharina Berens).

82. R 1:238; N 2:53. See Matthew 3:9.

83. ZH 5:207.

84. ZH 3:263. Though Hegel does not refer to it, Hamann's *Essay of a Sibyl on Marriage* is relevant in this context.

85. R 3:183–85; ZH 2:190–92.

86. R 3:207–8; ZH 2:225–26.

87. ZH 2:231–32.

88. N 2:135. See also note 7 above.

89. ZH 2:21. Throughout this essay, I have translated Hamann's *Muße* as "leisure" and his (and Hegel's) *lange Weile* or *Langeweile* as "boredom" (as in the subtitle of *Socratic Memorabilia*). See O'Flaherty, *Socratic Memorabilia,* 68.

90. R 3:296–97, 299–300; ZH 2:261–62, 268. See also Goethe, *From My Life,* 380.

91. R 5:18; ZH 3:17–18. It seems that Kant had urged his friend Johann Konrad Jacobi (1717–74) to help secure this post for Hamann. See Kuehn, *Kant: A Biography,* 165.

92. ZH 3:72.

93. Hegel's page reference seems to be in error. The letters at R 5:166ff. are concerned with the death of Lindner and not at all with Moser or Hamann's financial situation. Hegel is likely thinking of R 5:62; ZH 3:75, where Hamann subtly indicates in a letter to Herder that Moser has "fulfilled all my expectations." For the nickname Hamann uses to mask Moser's identity there, see R 3:202; ZH 2:219.

94. R 5:183, 186–87; ZH 3:250, 257–58.

95. N 3:141. What Hegel calls a *Letter to the Public* here is actually one of Hamann's *Hierophantic Letters.*

96. ZH 3:301–3. *Foigelder* refers to a levy imposed on the shippers, initially distributed among the civil servants, but later directed instead into the royal coffers (another source of Hamann's bitterness).

97. Johann Friedrich Reichardt (1752–1814), director of the symphony orchestra in Berlin. The letters are found at R 5:220–36; ZH 3:311–16, 340–44.

98. R 5:290–91, 222; ZH 4:31, 3:312.

99. ZH 4:25.

100. ZH 3:296.

101. ZH 4:301, 336.

102. R 6:178–225; ZH 4:278–349. In addition to Hamann's reading of Voltaire, Kant, Locke, and Herder, Hegel refers to Ange Goudar's (1720–91) *Trial of the Three Kings,* a critical parody of relations between Britain and America; the Freemason and theosophist Louis Claude de Saint-Martin's (1743–1803) *Of Errors and Truth* (1775); Mouffle d'Angerville's (1728–95) *The Private Life of Louis XV* (1781); the work of the French naturalist Georges Louis Leclerc (1707–88) on birds; and the Protestant theologian Gustav Georg Zeltner's (1672–1738) *Historia* (1729).

103. ZH 4:7. Johann Kaspar Lavater (1741–1801) was a Swiss poet and physiognomist.

104. See, for example, R 5:157, 190; ZH 3:205, 260.

105. In this autobiographical work from 1778, the German writer Theodor Gottlieb von Hippel (1741–96) originally meant to portray the lives of his father and grandfather as well.

106. Both Johann Gottlieb Kreutzfeld (1745–84) and Christian Jacob Kraus (1753–1807) were close friends of Hamann's and students of Kant's.

107. Johann Georg Scheffner (1736–1820) was a friend of both Hamann and Kant. Hegel refers rather critically to Scheffner's *My Life as Described by Me* (1816).

108. ZH 1:338.

109. R 1:474–75; ZH 1:405–6.

110. ZH 6:222.

111. ZH 3:74, 96, 127.

112. In 1769 the Academy of Sciences in Berlin announced its intention to give a prize for the best essay on the origin of languages. Herder's treatise won the prize. In Goethe's words, Hamann's critique of the treatise, "in a most individual way, illuminates this Herderian specimen with strange sidelights" (Goethe, *From My Life*, 380). Hamann's critique is found at R 4:6–11; N 3:17–24.

113. N 3:35–53.

114. R 4:48–49; N 3:41–42.

115. R 6:47–54; N 3:275–80. It seems this notice went unpublished for fear that it would injure Kant. It did not appear until 1801.

116. Colette suggests that Hegel means the *Socratic Memorabilia* (Colette, *Hegel*, 133, note 106).

117. R 1:395; ZH 1:341.

118. The phrase *die Stillen im Lande* is taken directly from the Luther translation of Psalm 35:20, via Goethe's autobiography (379). It has historically been used to refer to Pietists and other Protestant groups.

119. A text written in 1761 which Hamann subtitled his "sequel" to the *Socratic Memorabilia*.

120. The language Hegel uses to describe these images is clearly taken from that used by Goethe in *From My Life*. Goethe further notes that the latter image "was intended as a lampoon against certain types of church music" (380). For both images, see N 2:113, 128.

121. ZH 1:320. See Psalm 139:14.

122. The passage Hegel is paraphrasing actually begins at R 1:392, where Hamann writes: "How solemnly the Apostle, in his first epistle, delivered a sinner unto Satan for the destruction of the flesh," referencing 1 Corinthians 5:5, which continues, "that the spirit may be saved in the day of the Lord Jesus." Hamann continues at R 1:393: "What a mixture of passions this achieved in the minds of Paul as well as the Corinthians? . . . Responsibility, anger, fear, desire, zeal, vengeance. If natural man has five senses, then the Christian is an instrument with ten strings and, *without passions*, resembles a clanging more than a new man." See 2 Corinthians 7:11 and 1 Corinthians 13:1. Taken together, these references would imply that the "mixture of passions" being exchanged between Berens, Lindner, and Hamann are all a necessary result of Hamann's attempt, in the Pauline role, to "save the spirit" of his friends.

123. The physician Gottlob Immanuel Lindner (1734–1808), younger brother of Hamann's good friend J. G. Lindner, was the author of *New Views About Several Metaphysical, Moral, and Religious Systems and Doctrines*, published by Nicolovius in 1817.

124. R 3:ix.

125. ZH 3:349–50.

126. Friedrich Leopold zu Stolberg-Stolberg (1750–1819) was a German writer and a member of the Göttinger Hain circle.

127. Ecclesiastes 9:7, 9.

128. ZH 4:5. Where Hegel has "*knots of doubt*" (*Zweifelknoten*), Hamann actually writes "*worlds of doubt*" (*Zweifelwelten*).

129. Greek for "the very image of those things"; see Hebrews 10:1.

130. 1 Corinthians 13:12.

131. Greek for "fulfilling" or "fulfillment."

132. ZH 4:6. See 1 Corinthians 13:10.

133. Hegel mistakenly has "J. G." Lindner here.

134. R 3:viii–ix. Lindner refers to Prosper Jolyot de Crébillon (1674–1762), French poet and dramatist.

135. Romans 3:29.

136. ZH 7:172. Karl Friedrich Bahrdt was the author of a *System of Moral Theology* (1770) and *Letters on Systematic Theology* (1770–72).

137. Hegel mistakenly references R 1:x, but he is paraphrasing what Roth writes on page viii.

138. Hamann refers to this critique quite specifically at the beginning of his "response," *Clouds*. See R 2:53; N 2:85.

139. Including *Aesthetica in nuce*.

140. The *Briefe, die neueste Literatur betreffend* (*Letters on the Most Recent Literature*), as the full title read, was edited and published by Gotthold Ephraim Lessing, Moses Mendelssohn, and Friedrich Nicolai from 1759 to 1765. During this time, the periodical was among the most important intellectual journals in Germany.

141. R 6:27–35; N 3:232–37. Friedrich Gottlieb Klopstock (1724–1803) is less familiar for his reformative studies of language than for his *Messiah* (1748).

142. R 4:257, 7:120; N 3:149, 399. In what became known as the "crypto-Catholicism debate," allegations were made in the *Berliner Monatsschrift* (*Berlin Monthly*) and the *Allgemeine Deutsche Bibliothek* that Johann Christian Starck (1741–1816), a Freemason and a former member of a Jesuit order which had been banned, continued to practice proselytization of a Catholic and Masonic nature among Protestants. Starck, the author of an *Apology of the Order of Freemasons* (1778), later broke with Freemasonry and wrote against it, but not before bringing an eventually unsuccessful defamation suit against the leaders of the Berlin Enlightenment. See ZH 7:418–19. For a more detailed analysis of the crypto-Catholicism issue in the context of Hamann's Lutheranism, see Fritz Blanke, *Hamann-Studien* (Zürich: Zwingli, 1956), 43–68. Nadler further suggests that Hamann's *Konxompax: Fragments of an Apocryphal Sibyl About Apocalyptic Mysteries* (1779) was occasioned by both Starck's *Apology* and Christoph Meiners's *On the Mysteries of the Ancients* (1776). See Nadler, *Johann Georg Hamann*, 322–23.

143. R 4:97–101; N 3:111–14. Johann August Eberhard's *Apology of Socrates* was published in 1788.

144. Charles Guichard (1724–75), called Quintus Icilius, was the author of the military treatise *Mémoires militaires sur les Grecs et les Romains* (1758) and a favorite of Frederick II.

145. R 4:149–68, 201–10; N 2:299–326.

146. See, for example, R 8:232; N 3:390, 5:369; ZH 7:159.

147. With Frederick II in dire need of funds after the Seven Years' War, East Prussia had come under French tax administration (the French having perfected the art of exorbitant taxation) in 1766. While it necessitated his position as an official translator, this also became one of the most vocal of Hamann's many criticisms of Frederick II. For a detailed analysis of all these criticisms, see O'Flaherty, *Quarrel of Reason*, 129–43.

148. Mendelssohn's book and Hamann's critical response to it appeared in 1783 and 1784, respectively. Hegel will return to *Golgotha and Sheblimini* later in his review. The text of *Golgotha and Sheblimini* is found at R 7:17–70; N 3:291–320.

149. ZH 1:344. See 2 Corinthians 2:14.

150. R 1:395–96; ZH 1:343. In Numbers 22, Bileam (or Balaam) is riding on a donkey which sees the angel of the Lord and refuses to keep walking. "Then the Lord opened the mouth of the donkey" (22:28) and thus "the eyes of Balaam" (22:31). Hamann also refers to the donkey in his *Last Will and Testament of the Knight of the Rose-Cross on the Divine and Human Origin of Language,* as an example of "a higher being, or an angel . . . wanting to work through our tongues" (R 4:24; N 3:27).

151. The Roth edition has *"Lügen-, Schau-* und *Mautpropheten"*; Hegel points out in the body of his text that Hamann probably intended "prophets of the mouth" (*Maulpropheten*), as opposed to those of the heart, and that has been corrected or adopted in newer editions. See ZH 3:67.

152. In a passage of the *Socratic Memorabilia* which Hegel does not directly discuss, Hamann notes that Alcibiades once (in Plato's *Symposium*) compared Socrates' parables to "certain sacred figures of the gods and goddesses, which were carried, according to the custom of the time, in a small case [*Gehäuse*], upon which one saw nothing but the image of a goat-footed satyr" (R 2:46–47; N 2:80). Hamann would seem to be complaining to Moser then, in this letter, that his own critics are, perhaps like Hegel here, more concerned with the external form of his writings than with that which is hidden within them. Hegel's parenthetical note uses the term "silene" rather than "satyr," but the two are often used interchangeably.

153. ZH 3:67. Where Hegel, following an error in the Roth edition, refers to the *façon* "of the sentence or the plan" (*des Satzes oder Plans*), Hamann's letter actually has "the satyr or Pan" (*des Satyrs oder Pans*). I have not been able to track down the final reference to the murder of popes and Turks.

154. N 3:403–7. The Hebrew *schew-limini,* "be seated at my right," is found in Psalm 110:1: "The Lord says to my lord, 'Sit at my right hand until I make your enemies your footstool.'" Sichem or Shechem was for a time the holy city of the Samaritans.

155. N 3:312.

156. I am indebted to John McCumber ("Hegel and Hamann," 78) for his interpretation of this exceedingly difficult Hegelian sentence.

157. On these divisions, see Dunning, *Tongues of Men*, 105.

158. Moses Mendelssohn, *Jerusalem, or On Religious Power and Judaism,* trans. Allan Arkush (Hanover: Brandeis University Press, 1983), 46–48. See also

Dunning, *Tongues of Men*, 141, 158, for Hamann's interpretation of Mendelssohn here.

159. I have followed here Arkush's English translation of Mendelssohn (*Jerusalem*, 40), the "wordiness" of which seems to me necessary in order to render accurately these rich terminologies. Hegel stays quite close here to Mendelssohn's language.

160. Mendelssohn, *Jerusalem*, 44–45.

161. N 3:296, 303. Hamann goes on to say that such bisection renders the state "a body without spirit and life," and the church a "ghost without flesh and bones" (R 7:40; N 3:303).

162. N 3:281–89.

163. Friedrich Theodor Rink (1770–1811) and Gottlob Benjamin Jäsche (1762–1842) published the volume in Königsberg. Bayer points out that the term *metacritique*, applied to Hamann, can have a number of different meanings. In the strictest sense, it refers to the particular text about Kant's *Critique of Pure Reason* written in 1784. Less strictly applied, it would refer to the phase of Hamann's thought spanning the period 1780–84. In its broadest sense, Bayer says, *metacritique* refers to Hamann's general method of reading. See Oswald Bayer, "Die Geschichten der Vernunft sind die Kritik ihrer Reinheit: Hamanns Weg zur Metakritik Kants," in *Hamann—Kant—Herder*, 9; and Bayer, *Vernunft ist Sprache*.

164. Herder's *Metacritique on the Critique of Pure Reason* was published in 1799.

165. R 7:5–6; N 3:284.

166. Hamann was in the habit of using the phrase as an epithet for Kant himself. See Betz, "Enlightenment Revisited," 294.

167. For *leaven* as a symbol of the hypocritical teachings of Pharisees, see Matthew 16, Mark 8:15, and Luke 12:1. See also 1 Corinthians 5:7.

168. Claude Adrien Helvetius (1715–71) was a French philosopher, writer, and statesman. The question mark in the text is Hegel's; it is possible he misses Hamann's intended irony here. It is hard to believe that Hamann would deem wise the man originally responsible for the idea of the French-administered excise system implemented under Frederick II. See note 147 above.

169. R 7:6–8; N 3:284–85. Hegel's final quotation here is mostly accurate, but he leaves out the phrase "of ideal relations" after "sheer hieroglyphics and types." For the empty wineskin, see ZH 7:172. *Losung* can mean both "watchword" and "droppings"; both meanings are certainly intended.

170. R 7:9–10; N 3:286. For the divorce of what nature has joined together, see Matthew 19:6. The same reference predominates in much of *Golgotha and Sheblimini* as well. See also ZH 7:158.

171. R 7:11; N 3:287. The Tree of Diana refers, in alchemy, to a dendrite made with silver and mercury, silver being associated with Diana. The tree imagery is borrowed from Kant's *Critique;* see Immanuel Kant, *Critique of Pure Reason*, ed. and trans. Paul Guyer and Allen W. Wood (Cambridge: Cambridge University Press, 1998), 213. Hamann then allies Kant and his philosophy with Newton and metals by making the tree in question an alchemical one, and then seems to reclaim the image for his own preference of *coincidentia oppositorum* rather than for Kantian divisions. Of course, with issues of knowledge and the limits thereof in question, al-

lusion to the biblical tree of the knowledge of good and evil (Genesis 2:17) is also intended. So the image allows Hamann to combine the pagan tradition, the Judeo-Christian one, and the task of contemporary philosophy.

172. See Dickson, *Hamann's Relational Metacriticism,* 179.

173. The word *galimatias* has come into English and German from the French, and means "confused language, meaningless talk, gibberish" (*Oxford English Dictionary*). Hamann also uses it in his *Essais à la Mosaique* (R 2:349; N 2:281), *Reader and Critic* (R 2:402; N 2:343), and his review of Herder (R 4:9; N 3:18).

174. For Hamann's wish for Demosthenes' eloquence, and the triunity which seems to puzzle Hegel, see R 6:355, 7:151; ZH 5:88, 177; N 2:247. For Demosthenes and action, see R 2:111, 3:64, 7:216; N 2:116; ZH 2:69, 5:359–60.

175. The ladder refers to that in Jacob's dream; see Genesis 28:12. The Hebrew *Mahanaim* translates to "two hosts"; see Genesis 32:1–2 and Song of Solomon 6:13. The latter verse also includes the designation "Shulamite" for the beloved of the Song.

176. In Greek mythology, Baubo exposed herself to Demeter in order to cheer her following the abduction of Persephone. Bayer suggests that Baubo "playing with herself" refers to the masturbatory nature, in Hamann's estimation, of Kantian pure reason, concerned ultimately with nothing but itself. See Bayer, "Geschichten der Vernunft," 35; and Bayer, *Vernunft ist Sprache,* 370–71, which includes a quotation from Hamann's source, Arnobius's *Adversus nationes.*

177. R 7:11–13; N 3:287. Bayer suggests that the final reference may be a general one to Mariology in the tradition of Anselm of Canterbury, or a specific one to his ontological proof of God's existence. See Bayer, *Vernunft ist Sprache,* 373.

178. R 7:13; N 3:288.

179. Greek for "Give me a place to stand . . . ," a reference to Archimedes' famous statement that concludes, ". . . and I shall move the earth." See Bayer, *Vernunft ist Sprache,* 407. See also ZH 5:333.

180. Greek for "first lie"; see Bayer, *Vernunft ist Sprache,* 405–13.

181. R 7:16; N 3:289. For the source of the balled fist/open hand image, the Stoic philosopher Zeno of Citium, see Bayer, *Vernunft ist Sprache,* 418–19.

182. ZH 4:285–87. See O'Flaherty, *Quarrel of Reason,* 27; Nadler, *Johann Georg Hamann,* 409.

183. The term *entfalten* means literally "to unfold," "to develop." I have chosen "unclench" as the translation which best corresponds to the very tangible image of the balled fist, but a shift in terminology seems necessary when Hegel extends the metaphor to God's hand and the *unfolding* or *development* of his truth. The multivalence of the German term *entfalten* means that all of these renderings are suggested, but the most common meaning, "develop," should also be borne in mind. Similarly, I have used "open hand" to render Hamann's "*flache Hand,*" as this phrase fits the image better in English than would "flat hand." Hegel, too, will use "open" (*offen*) rather than "flat" (*flach*) when speaking of God's hand in this context.

184. In Hegel, the juxtaposition between this "transcendence" (*über . . . hinauszugehen*) and this "entering into" (*in . . . hineinzugehen*) is more clearly delineated by the parallelism. The link is carried even further by the fact that "reflect-

ing *on*" uses the pronoun *über* in German, hearkening back to the theme of transcendence (also with the preposition *über*).

185. See McCumber, "Hegel and Hamann," 77.

186. Mendelssohn's original statement is found in vol. 3, part 15, page 172 of the *Literaturbriefe* (254th letter). Hamann's comment is at N 2:257.

187. N 3:126–27; ZH 3:120. This reference and the following one come from Hamann's *Prolegomena on the Newest Interpretation of the Oldest Document of the Human Race*.

188. N 3:133. For the letter to Herder in which Hamann explains "Mamamuschi," see R 5:114–15; ZH 3:130. Johann Jacob Kanter (1738–86) was well known, among other things, for his paper mill in Trutenau. He also owned a bookshop in Königsberg (from which Hamann frequently borrowed) from which he published and distributed the *Königsberger Zeitung* (1764–96) that Hegel frequently mentions.

189. N 3:98. Again the explanation for this is found in the letter to Herder at R 5:114; ZH 3:130. See also R 2:385; N 2:334, 6:339. It was probably the refusal of these city officials to hire Hamann to the positions for which he had applied there that invited these remarks. See Rosenkranz, "Hamann und Kant," 40.

190. Mendelssohn uses this phrase ("im Stande der Natur") to distinguish from the state of society ("im Stande der Gesellschaft"). See pages 35–52 in Arkush's *Jerusalem* translation.

191. For an interpretation of the reference to the three biblical kings, see Dunning, *Tongues of Men*, 92–93 and 107–8, where especially the parallel between Nimrod and Frederick II clarifies Hamann's criticism.

192. Hamann is referring here to the maturity (*Mündigkeit*) to which the reader is exhorted in Kant's "Answer to the Question: What Is Enlightenment?" (1783), a text which Hamann excoriates, claiming to lay bare Kant's pretension to tolerance and his hypocrisy, in a 1784 letter to Kraus. See Schmidt, *What Is Enlightenment?* The reference makes clear that it is not only Mendelssohn (the passage comes from Hamann's discussion, in *Golgotha and Sheblimini*, of the social contract examined in *Jerusalem*) in his admiration of Frederick II, but also Kant who is understood to be, among other things, the "lap dog" of Frederick II. On Hamann's response to Kant's "What Is Enlightenment?" see Betz, "Enlightenment Revisited," 295–99; and Bayer, *Vernunft ist Sprache*, 427–68.

193. Hegel mistakenly has the reference as Job 40:18.

194. R 7:32–33; N 3:299–300.

195. R 7:166; ZH 5:217. See also ZH 6:204.

196. Goethe, *From My Life*, 379–81. Again, Hegel's wording here is extremely similar to that of Goethe's autobiography. Goethe's admission of Hamann's influence on his early career is likely one of the origins of the common reference to Hamann as the father of the Sturm und Drang movement.

197. Hegel seems to be paraphrasing rather than actually quoting here. See Mendelssohn's 254th letter in the *Literaturbriefe*, 172–73, 186–88.

198. R 2:493; N 2:263. It is Hegel's parenthetical note that specifies Voltaire, one of Hamann's favorite targets. The German for Voltaire's "product" (*Gemächt*) also carries the connotation of its alternate meaning, referring to genitalia. While

the "adulterous people" refers, in connection with Voltaire, to the French, the mention of the "calf" also evokes associations with the disobedient Israelites (see Exodus 32 and the golden calf). The reference comes from Hamann's *Crusades of a Philologian,* which is in its entirety concerned with the question of taste (*Geschmack*).

199. Hegel takes Mendelssohn's words here almost verbatim. See the 254th letter in the *Literaturbriefe,* 174.

200. Hegel is likely thinking of some of the more humorous parts of Hippel's *Lives in an Ascending Line* (see note 105) as well as his comedy *The Man of the Clock* (1766).

201. R 4:vi and Friedrich Heinrich Jacobi, *Werke,* ed. Friedrich Roth and Friedrich Köppen (Darmstadt: Wissenschaftliche Buchgesellschaft, 1968), vol. 4, part 2, page 264.

202. In fact, Goethe was introduced to Hamann's work by Herder, who of course "set great store by" it, but "usually merely found it amusing when I [Goethe] made some no doubt very odd attempts to understand these sibylline pages. But I nevertheless felt that something in Hamann's writings appealed to me, and I yielded to it without knowing whence it came or whither it led" (Goethe, *From My Life,* 303).

203. R 7:71–128; N 3:347–407.

204. ZH 6:336.

205. R vol. 8, part 1, pages 355–93. The Nadler edition presents the first and second versions side by side on pages 3:347–407.

206. ZH 6:239. See Judges 15:15. The review had been published anonymously.

207. R 7:78–80; N 3:353–57.

208. R 7:99, 113; ZH 3:377, 391. The "Public German Jezebel" and the "Alemannish Place of the Skull" are derogatory designations for the journal *Allgemeine Deutsche Bibliothek* (see note 5 above), the former presumably because of her generally unfavorable reputation, the latter because the journal, like Golgotha, became in Hamann's eyes a place of critical "executions." The title page of the *Allgemeine Deutsche Bibliothek* showed the head of Homer. See N 6:199–200, 335. Presumably, the rest of this passage consists of further criticism of the *Allgemeine Deutsche Bibliothek.*

209. R 7:107; N 3:385. See note 71 above.

210. R 7:113; N 3:391–93. According to Nadler, the "brothers" actually refer to the two elders who bore false witness against the virtuous Susanna in the biblical story (N 6:370). Belial is an evil spirit often identified with Satan.

211. See, for example, ZH 7:157.

212. For the biblical references in this passage, see Job 36:26, Isaiah 8:6, and Job 13:25. Most translations of Job 13:25 use "windblown leaf" or something of the sort for Luther's "fliegend Blatt," which Hamann adopts, but "flying page" retains the connection to Hamann's "Flying Letter" (*Fliegender Brief*).

213. Matthew 11:16–17, 29; 12:42.

214. Psalm 133:2.

215. N 3:339–401. Hegel mistakenly references page 120 in the Roth edition. See Matthew 26:6–13; Mark 14:3–9; John 12.

216. See Dunning, *Tongues of Men*, 128.

217. R 7:375; ZH 7:283.

218. Goethe's biography, though filled with praise for Herder, also notes his "contradictory spirit" and "changes of mood" (Goethe, *From My Life*, 299–300).

219. R 7:383; ZH 7:314–15. See also Ecclesiastes 1:2 and *Socratic Memorabilia*, R 2:32; N 2:71.

220. ZH 7:135. Hippel was the mayor of Königsberg from 1778 to 1781.

221. ZH 7:152.

222. ZH 7:236. Nadler points out that Hamann did begin using the informal *du* address with Jacobi (making him unique among Hamann's friends) rather early in their correspondence (Nadler, *Johann Georg Hamann*, 365).

223. See R 7:185–86, 196; ZH 5:283–85, 298.

224. Johann Friedrich Hartknoch (1740–89) was a Riga bookseller and publisher of many of Kant's works.

225. R 7:319; ZH 6:468.

226. Hegel fails to mention that the Baroness Bondelli was an old friend of Hamann's with whom he had visited and corresponded. Hamann had long referred to her as "my oldest woman friend [*Freundin*]." This seems to have been a situation not altogether different from Buchholtz's offering of financial assistance for the education of Hamann's children. See R 7:198–99; ZH 5:334–35.

227. Jean-François Marmontel (1723–99) was a French critic, dramatist, and contributor to Diderot's *Encyclopédie*.

228. See ZH 5:445–46, 6:369.

229. Hamann's third request is found at ZH 7:143–46. The text of the letter he received in response, the one Hegel excerpts, is at ZH 7:161, and also at 7:189–90 when Hamann forwards it to Jacobi.

230. ZH 7:211.

231. See ZH 7:200–210.

232. Hamann left the Buchholtz family for a time so as not to burden them while Buchholtz's wife Marianne was expecting a child. He returned to them from Jacobi's once the child had been born. See R 7:385; ZH 7:319.

233. ZH 7:248.

234. Princess Adelheid Amalia von Gallitzin (1748–1806) was an often devout adherent of Catholicism and a great admirer of Hamann's. Her good friend Franz Friedrich von Fürstenberg (1729–1810) was a Münster statesman and pedagogical reformer.

235. See the letters Hegel cites below from Jacobi to Lavater.

236. ZH 7:271. The friend to whom Hamann wrote was Sophie Marianne Courtan.

237. See R 7:421; ZH 7:494.

238. ZH 7:445, 461. Johann Michael Sailer (1751–1832) was a Jesuit priest and later bishop who authored a prayer book for Catholics. See also note 142 above.

239. ZH 7:377.

240. Hamann used this particular nickname to evoke the especially close friendship between David and Jonathan. See 2 Samuel 1:26.

241. For Hamann's criticism of Jacobi's *On the Teaching of Spinoza in Letters to Herr Moses Mendelssohn* (1785) and especially his *David Hume on Faith, or Idealism and Realism: A Dialogue* (1787), including that which Hegel will continue to detail, see ZH 7:156–60.

242. According to ZH 7:160, what Hamann actually says about nature and reason is that they "are as much *correlata* as they are *opposita*," as "*faire et confondre* applies equally to both." Skepticism and dogmatism, Hamann continues, "can stand just as suitably alongside each other as knowledge and ignorance (and doubt with them both), as αντιθεσεις τῆς ψευδωνυμου γνωσεως [oppositions of science falsely so called] with the *plerophoria* of judgment and will, as tares with the wheat, as the change of hours and seasons with the regular course of nature." For the phrase Hamann quotes in Greek, see 1 Timothy 6:20. For *plerophoria* as "full assurance," see Colossians 2:2. See also ZH 7:165–66, 174.

243. ZH 7:175–76. Hamann actually calls Spinoza "the poor rogue of Cartesian *Diabolo* and cabbalistic somnambulists, from whom Leibniz supposedly stole his *Harm. praestab.*" He continues: "Can there be a conceivable difference between *essence* and existence? Can there be a *Causa* without *Effect* or vice-versa? Are there absolute things for relative concepts? Ναφε και μιμνας απιστειν [Be sober of head and mistrustful of] all such chimeras, words and *signs de mauvaises plaisanteries* of mathematical fiction for the arbitrary constructions of philosophical primers and bibles, whose paltry elements are to understand the revealed word but not the key of the meaning, of the concept, as *charades* are definitions of a word." The Greek phrase Hamann borrows from the epigraph Jacobi had given his dialogue on idealism and realism, which Jacobi in turn took from Epicharmos's *Trochaic Fragments*. (The translation is E. O. Winstedt's.) Hamann alters the context of the citation significantly in his letter, however. The full text of Jacobi's epigraph warns one to be "mistrustful of friends." See Friedrich Heinrich Jacobi, *The Main Philosophical Writings and the Novel Allwill*, ed. and trans. George di Giovanni (Montreal: McGill-Queen's University Press, 1994), 253, note 605.

244. ZH 7:166. Hamann actually wrote to Jacobi that "the *talisman* of your philosophy and your *superstition* in *verba praetereaque nihil* are the idols of your concepts, just as Spinoza imagined the letter to be the word and the master of the work."

245. ZH 7:451, 412. The Dutch philosopher Frans Hemsterhuis was a member of Gallitzin's circle, and was actually the first to use the nickname "Diotima" for her. See Nadler, *Johann Georg Hamann*, 425.

246. ZH 7:156.

247. Hegel is referring to a 1788 dialogue which Jacobi published in the *Deutsches Museum* (*German Museum*), in the midst of the crypto-Catholicism debate. See note 142 above. Hamann's critical response is found at ZH 7:475.

248. ZH 7:212.

249. ZH 7:456.

250. R 7:421–22; ZH 7:442, 494–95.

251. ZH 7:264.

252. ZH 7:405–6. Hamann references two parables of rejoicing, in which a shepherd finds a lost sheep (Matthew 18:12–13; Luke 15:4–6), and a woman a lost

coin (Luke 15:8–9). The last phrase, "nicht aus Verdienst und Würdigkeit," is one Hamann uses repeatedly in one form or another (see, for example, R 4:41; N 3:37–38) and seems to have come from Luther's *Little Catechism,* with its reference to the fact that God's goodness and mercy are based on neither merit nor worth.

253. Friedrich Heinrich Jacobi, *Auserlesener Briefwechsel,* ed. Friedrich Roth (Leipzig: Fleischer, 1825–27), 1:486.

254. See, for example, R 7:421–27; ZH 7: 494–96.

255. ZH 7:285.

256. R 7:391; ZH 7:327.

257. I have not been able to locate this exact quote in Hamann's letters. It is possible that Hegel is paraphrasing what Hamann writes in September 1787; see R 7:378; ZH 7:288–89.

258. ZH 7:316–18.

259. R 7:394; ZH 7:344. See also R 7:386–89; ZH 7:320, 324.

260. Hamann seems to be casting himself and *Jacobi's* sisters into the roles of the biblical siblings Lazarus, Mary, and Martha (see John 11). See the section "'Bruder Jonathan': Jacobi" in the introductory essay in this volume, as well as ZH 7:426.

261. ZH 7:337–38. See Jacobi's response at ZH 7:354. Hegel makes two important omissions in quoting this letter of November 17, 1787. The entirety of the passage reads:

> But you, poor Jonathan, have done us wrong, your two sisters and me, Lazarus, *quoad tunc,* in burdening their sex, which nature made softer and tamer, with the hard yoke and the heavy burden of such a *masculine* friendship, such a *holy* landscape as that which presides over us. You caused me many a sour and difficult hour, having to forgive this civil error [*Staatsfehler*] you committed, this hindrance in the calculation of my plan. Just as soon as I was back on my feet, thanks to the care I enjoyed in your house (which surely works most quickly and vigorously on our organs and their recovery naturally through the most appropriate *means*), I needed those hours to escape the danger with a sort of *paroxysmo.* Have you not noticed, then, dear Jonathan, that these two Amazons had made it a point to conspire to deprive me, poor old man, of the honor of my whole philosophy, of all of your favorable judgments thereof, on which your friendship has been based, and finally to bring us both into such embarrassment that we would have seemed ridiculous to each other and even to ourselves, like a couple of *philosophical ghosts?*

262. ZH 7:368. Hegel calls this Hamann's "next" letter to Jacobi after the one in which he takes Jacobi and his sisters to task, but in fact a few more came between. The text of Hamann's letter reads:

> The love which I enjoyed in your house and from your relatives bears no relationship to my merit. I have been taken up into it like an angel of heaven. Had I been an incarnate son of *Zeus* or *Hermes,* I could not have found a greater sacrifice of hospitality and generous self-denial than that in which *Mama,* as

your and my neighbor, has immortally distinguished herself. Her good deeds are and will remain unforgettable in my memory and emotions as long as I live. If I care for my health (and who does not love the *best good of his life?*), then I know and am convinced that I owe the greatest part of my recovery to your care and tireless diligence and self-denial. Should I now attribute this effort and exaggeration of sympathy simply to my needs, rather than to your partiality of friendship for me, and arrogate something which belonged more to you than to me?

Hamann, always prone to using nicknames, used "Mama" to refer to Jacobi's sister Helene. See ZH 7:302.

263. See ZH 7:369.

264. Hegel becomes somewhat imprecise about letters and dates here. The letter of November 17 is the one in which Hamann originally chastises Jacobi and his sisters. The letter in which he has just been praising Jacobi and his sister Helene is from December 6. Now Hegel returns to the letter of November 17.

265. ZH 7:334–37.

266. ZH 7:432, 508–9.

Appendix

Hegel's notebook entries include "Notes on Hamann (1828)," the text of which is translated in this appendix. I am grateful to the Felix Meiner Verlag for their permission to include a translation of all the material in this appendix and its note (which appears below). Both were originally published in G. W. F. Hegel, *Berliner Schriften,* ed. Johannes Hoffmeister (Hamburg: Felix Meiner, 1956), 694–95.

1. Hegel has another notebook entry entitled "[On Philipp Matthäus] Hahn's (A Pastor in Echterdingen) *Posthumous Works,* Heilbronn 1828," which reads as follows:

First Part. His own biography:

Page 5. "At confirmation and at the Holy Supper, I received especially *serious impressions.* I asked God to crush my hardness, to soften my heart, to prepare penance in me and to give me faith. But I felt no success. Sure, I came through with the Ten Commandments . . . but I was in need, and when I went anyway to the Supper had no feeling of my sins, nor of the grace of God and reconciliation through Christ. I believed that I had received the Supper undeservingly; only I found in a prayer book, if one believes he has received the Supper undeservingly, then he has only to pray earnestly to God.

. . . Hereafter the sins of my youth, and the attractions of unchastity which grew stronger with increased age—and I was always afraid during thunderstorms and at night, and finally unseemly thoughts of God—all this discouraged me so much that I saw myself as the greatest of sinners."

Page 11. "What I liked about the 'hours of edification' of the Pietists was that they spoke in such a childlike manner, so open-heartedly about the impressions which the Word of God had made upon them, about their misery in sin and about the grace of God through Christ which they had experienced, how they loved each other as brothers, awakened themselves through song and heartfelt prayers to further earnestness . . ."

Page 12. "I respected the Pietists without engaging in a closer association with them, because I could not yet speak with them, and went walking instead with other students who did not go to the hours of edification . . ."

[Hegel]: The one-sided, eternal monotony of sin and grace is surely good for beginners, for upon this foundation a Christian must begin to build; but there are still several more truths which belong to the entire Gospel.

Selected Bibliography

This is, of course, only a sampling of the many books and articles available on Hegel, Hamann, their contemporaries, and friendship. I list here only the most important works and those cited in this volume. For present purposes, I focus also more upon secondary works in English than in German.

Primary Sources in German

Hamann, Johann Georg. *Briefwechsel*. Edited by Walther Ziesemer and Arthur Henkel. 7 vols. Frankfurt: Insel, 1955–75.
———. *Sämtliche Werke*. Edited by Josef Nadler. 6 vols. Vienna: Herder, 1949–57.
———. *Schriften*. Edited by Friedrich Roth. 8 vols. Berlin: Reimer, 1821–43.
———. *Schriften*. Gallica, La Bibliothèque Numérique, Bibliothèque National de France. http://gallica.bnf.fr/Catalogue/noticesInd/FRBNF30571793.htm (accessed January 2, 2008).
Hegel, Georg Wilhelm Friedrich. *Sämtliche Werke*. Edited by Hermann Glockner. 20 vols. Stuttgart: F. Frommann, 1927–40.
———. *Sämtliche Werke: Neue kritische Ausgabe*. Edited by Johannes Hoffmeister. Incomplete edition. Hamburg: Felix Meiner, 1952–56.
———. *Werke*. Edited by Eva Moldenhauer and Karl Markus Michel. 20 vols. Frankfurt: Suhrkamp, 1969–71.
———. *Werke: Vollständige Ausgabe durch einen Verein von Freunden des Verewigten*. Edited by Philipp Marheineke et al. 18 vols. Berlin: Duncker und Humblot, 1832–45.

Primary Sources in English (Translations, Commentaries)

Dickson, Gwen Griffith. *Johann Georg Hamann's Relational Metacriticism*. New York: De Gruyter, 1995.
Hamann, Johann Georg. "Letter to Christian Jacob Kraus." Translated and annotated by Garrett Green in *What Is Enlightenment? Eighteenth-Century Answers and Twentieth-Century Questions*, edited by James B. Schmidt, 145–53. Berkeley: University of California Press, 1996.

———. "Metacritique on the Purism of Reason." Translated and annotated by Kenneth Haynes in *What Is Enlightenment? Eighteenth-Century Answers and Twentieth-Century Questions,* edited by James B. Schmidt, 154–67. Berkeley: University of California Press, 1996.

———. *Socratic Memorabilia: A Translation and Commentary.* Translated and edited by James C. O'Flaherty. Baltimore: Johns Hopkins University Press, 1967.

———. *Writings on Philosophy and Language.* Translated and edited by Kenneth Haynes. Cambridge: Cambridge University Press, 2007.

Smith, Ronald Gregor. *J. G. Hamann: A Study in Christian Existence, with Selections from His Writings.* New York: Harper, 1960.

Secondary Sources in German

Achermann, Eric. *Worte und Werte: Geld und Sprache bei Gottfried Wilhelm Leibniz, Johann Georg Hamann und Adam Müller.* Tübingen: Niemeyer, 1997.

Bayer, Oswald. "Die Geschichten der Vernunft sind die Kritik ihrer Reinheit. Hamanns Weg zur Metakritik Kants." In *Hamann—Kant—Herder: Acta des vierten Internationalen Hamann-Kolloquiums im Herder-Institut zu Marburg/Lahn 1985,* edited by Bernhard Gajek, 9–81. Frankfurt: Peter Lang, 1987.

———. *Johann Georg Hamann: Der hellste Kopf seiner Zeit.* Tübingen: Attempo, 1998.

———. *Vernunft ist Sprache: Hamanns Metakritik Kants.* Stuttgart: Frommann-Holzboog, 2002.

———. *Zeitgenosse im Widerspruch: Johann Georg Hamann als radikaler Aufklärer.* Munich: Piper, 1988.

Bayer, Oswald, Bernhard Gajek, and Josef Simon, eds. *Hamann.* Frankfurt: Insel, 1987.

Blanke, Fritz. *Hamann-Studien.* Zürich: Zwingli, 1956.

Gründer, Karlfried. "Hamann in Münster." In *Johann Georg Hamann,* edited by Reiner Wild, 264–98. Darmstadt: Wissenschaftliche Buchgesellschaft, 1978.

———. "Nachspiel zu Hegels Hamann-Rezension." *Hegel-Studien* 1 (1961): 81–101.

Jørgensen, Sven-Aage. *Johann Georg Hamann.* Stuttgart: Metzler, 1976.

Knoll, Renate. *Johann Georg Hamann und Friedrich Heinrich Jacobi.* Heidelberg: Winter, 1963.

Nadler, Josef. *Johann Georg Hamann: Der Zeuge des Corpus mysticum.* Salzburg: Otto Müller, 1949.

Nadler, Käte. "Hamann und Hegel: Zum Verhältnis von Dialektik und Existentialität." *Logos: Internationale Zeitschrift für Philosophie der Kultur* 20 (1931): 259–85.

Rosenkranz, Karl. "Hamann und Kant: Eine Parallele." In *Johann Georg Hamann,* edited by Reiner Wild, 16–43. Darmstadt: Wissenschaftliche Buchgesellschaft, 1978.

Simon, Josef. "Spuren Hamanns bei Kant?" In *Hamann—Kant—Herder: Acta des vierten Internationalen Hamann-Kolloquiums im Herder-Institut zu Marburg/Lahn 1985,* edited by Bernhard Gajek, 89–110. Frankfurt: Peter Lang, 1987.

Unger, Rudolf. *Hamann und die Aufklärung: Studien zur Vorgeschichte des romantischen Geistes im 18. Jahrhundert.* Darmstadt: Wissenschaftliche Buchgesellschaft, 1963.

Wohlfart, Günter. *Denken der Sprache: Sprache und Kunst bei Vico, Hamann, Humboldt und Hegel.* Freiburg: Alber, 1984.

Secondary Sources in English

Alexander, W. M. *Johann Georg Hamann: Philosophy and Faith.* The Hague: Martinus Nijhoff, 1966.

Beiser, Frederick C. *The Fate of Reason: German Philosophy from Kant to Fichte.* Cambridge: Harvard University Press, 1987.

Berlin, Isaiah. *The Magus of the North: J. G. Hamann and the Origins of Modern Irrationalism.* New York: Farrar, Straus and Giroux, 1993.

———. *Three Critics of the Enlightenment: Vico, Hamann, Herder.* Princeton: Princeton University Press, 2000.

Betz, John R. "Enlightenment Revisited: Hamann as the First and Best Critic of Kant's Philosophy." *Modern Theology* 20, no. 2 (2004): 291–301.

Dunning, Stephen. *The Tongues of Men: Hegel and Hamann on Religious Language and History.* Missoula: Scholars, 1979.

German, Terence J. *Hamann on Language and Religion.* Oxford: Oxford University Press, 1981.

Kuehn, Manfred. *Kant: A Biography.* New York: Cambridge University Press, 2001.

Leibrecht, Walter. *God and Man in the Thought of Hamann.* Translated by James H. Stam and Martin H. Bertam. Philadelphia: Fortress, 1966.

Lowrie, Walter. *Johann Georg Hamann, an Existentialist.* Princeton: Princeton Theological Seminary, 1950.

McCumber, John. "Hegel and Hamann: Ideas and Life." In *Hegel and the Tradition,* edited by Michael Baur and John Russon, 77–92. Toronto: University of Toronto Press, 1997.

Milbank, John. "Knowledge: The Theological Critique of Philosophy in Hamann and Jacobi." In *Radical Orthodoxy: A New Theology,* edited by John Milbank, Catherine Pickstock, and Graham Ward, 21–37. London: Routledge, 1999.

O'Flaherty, James C. *Johann Georg Hamann.* Boston: Twayne, 1979.

———. *The Quarrel of Reason with Itself: Essays on Hamann, Nietzsche, Lessing and Michaelis.* Columbia: Camden House, 1988.

———. *Unity and Language: A Study in the Philosophy of Johann Georg Hamann.* Chapel Hill: University of North Carolina Press, 1952.

Schmitz, F. J. "The Problem of Individualism and the Crises in the Lives of Lessing and Hamann." *University of California Publications in Modern Philosophy* 27, no. 3 (October 1944): 125–48.

Vaughan, Larry. *Johann Georg Hamann: Metaphysics of Language and Vision of History*. Frankfurt: Peter Lang, 1989.

Sources in Other Languages

Colette, Jacques, trans. and ed. *Hegel: Les écrits de Hamann*. Paris: Éditions Aubier-Montaigne, 1981.
Giametta, Sossio. *Hamann nella considerazione di Hegel, Goethe, Croce: In appendice due scritti di Hegel su Hamann*. Naples: Bibliopolis, 1984.
Klossowski, Pierre. *Mage du nord: Johann Georg Hamann*. Montpellier: Fata Morgana, 1988.
———. *Les Méditations Bibliques de Hamann. Avec une étude de Hegel*. Paris: Éditions de Minuit, 1948.

Sources on Friendship

Aristotle. *The Nicomachean Ethics*. Translated by David Ross. Oxford: Oxford University Press, 1980.
Badhwar, Neera Kapur, ed. *Friendship: A Philosophical Reader*. Ithaca: Cornell University Press, 1993.
Derrida, Jacques. *The Politics of Friendship*. Translated by George Collins. London: Verso, 2005.
Fenves, Peter. "Politics of Friendship—Once Again." *Eighteenth-Century Studies* 32, no. 2 (1998–99): 133–55.
Foucault, Michel. *Fearless Speech*. Edited by Joseph Pearson. Los Angeles: Semiotext(e), 2001.
Hermand, Jost. *Freundschaft: Zur Geschichte einer sozialen Bindung*. Cologne: Böhlau, 2006.
Heuser, Magdalene. "'Das beständige Angedencken vertritt die Stelle der Gegenwart': Frauen und Freundschaften in Briefen der Frühaufklärung und Empfindsamkeit." In *Frauenfreundschaft—Männerfreundschaft: Literarische Diskurse im 18. Jahrhundert,* edited by Wolfram Mauser and Barbara Becker-Cantarino, 141–65. Tübingen: Niemeyer, 1991.
Lankheit, Klaus. *Das Freundschaftsbild der Romantik*. Heidelberg: Carl Winter Universitätsverlag, 1952.
Mauser, Wolfram, and Barbara Becker-Cantarino. "Vorwort." In *Frauenfreundschaft—Männerfreundschaft: Literarische Diskurse im 18. Jahrhundert,* edited by Wolfram Mauser and Barbara Becker-Cantarino, vii–x. Tübingen: Niemeyer, 1991.
Morgan, Diane. "Amical Treachery: Kant, Hamann, Derrida and the Politics of Friendship." *Angelaki: Journal of the Theoretical Humanities* 3, no. 3 (1998): 143–52.
Munzel, Felicitas. "Menschenfreundschaft: Friendship and Pedagogy in Kant." *Eighteenth-Century Studies* 32, no. 2 (1998–99): 247–59.

Rasch, Wolfdietrich. *Freundschaftskult und Freundschaftsbildung im deutschen Schrifttum des 18. Jahrhunderts.* Halle: Niemeyer, 1936.

Sørensen, Bengt Algot. "Freundschaft und Patriarchat im 18. Jahrhundert." In *Frauenfreundschaft—Männerfreundschaft: Literarische Diskurse im 18. Jahrhundert,* edited by Wolfram Mauser and Barbara Becker-Cantarino, 279–92. Tübingen: Niemeyer, 1991.

Vollhardt, Friedrich. "Freundschaft und Pflicht: Naturrechtliches Denken und literarisches Freundschaftsideal im 18. Jahrhundert." In *Frauenfreundschaft—Männerfreundschaft: Literarische Diskurse im 18. Jahrhundert,* edited by Wolfram Mauser and Barbara Becker-Cantarino, 293–309. Tübingen: Niemeyer, 1991.

Other Works Cited in This Volume

Biedermann, W. F. von. *Goethes Gespräche.* 5 vols. Leipzig: Biedermann, 1909–11.

Goethe, Johann Wolfgang von. *From My Life: Poetry and Truth: Parts One to Three.* Edited by Thomas P. Saine and Jeffrey L. Sammons, translated by Robert R. Heitner. New York: Suhrkamp, 1994.

Hamilton, Edith. *Mythology.* Boston: Little, Brown, 1942.

Hegel, G. W. F. *Lectures on the Philosophy of Religion.* Edited by Peter C. Hodgson, translated by R. F. Brown et al. 3 vols. Berkeley: University of California Press, 1984–87.

———. *The Phenomenology of Mind.* Edited and translated by J. B. Baillie. 2nd ed. New York: Humanities, 1977.

Jacobi, Friedrich Heinrich. *Auserlesener Briefwechsel.* Edited by Friedrich Roth. 2 vols. Leipzig: Fleischer, 1825–27.

———. *The Main Philosophical Writings and the Novel Allwill.* Edited and translated by George di Giovanni. Montreal: McGill-Queen's University Press, 1994.

———. *Werke.* Edited by Friedrich Roth and Friedrich Köppen. 6 vols. Darmstadt: Wissenschaftliche Buchgesellschaft, 1968.

Kant, Immanuel. *Critique of Pure Reason.* Edited and translated by Paul Guyer and Allen W. Wood. Cambridge: Cambridge University Press, 1998.

———. *Practical Philosophy.* Edited by Allen Wood, translated by Mary Gregor. Cambridge: Cambridge University Press, 1996.

Mendelssohn, Moses. *Jerusalem, or On Religious Power and Judaism.* Translated by Allan Arkush. Hanover: Brandeis University Press, 1983.

Nicolai, Friedrich, Gotthold Ephraim Lessing, and Moses Mendelssohn, eds. *Briefe, die neueste Literatur betreffend.* 4 vols. Hildesheim: Georg Olms Verlag, 1974.

Index

G. W. F. Hegel (1770–1831) was one of the leading German philosophers of the nineteenth century. He taught at the University of Heidelberg and the University of Berlin. His most important works are *The Phenomenology of Spirit* (1807) and the *Encyclopedia of the Philosophical Sciences* (1817).

Lisa Marie Anderson is an assistant professor in the Department of German at Hunter College, City University of New York. She resides in New York City and researches intersections between literature, religion, and philosophy in modern German culture.